# DATING A NIGHTMARE:
## Avoiding, Surviving and Escaping a Covert Narcissist

By

Aydin Guner

# ALSO BY THE AUTHOR

The Vengeful One: A Christmas Tale
The Devil In I
Behind the Mask: An Introduction into Covert Narcissism
10 Steps to Heal from Narcissistic Abuse

# DISCLAIMER

All use cases, characters and examples used in this book are 100% fictional and not based on anyone real.

# TABLE OF CONTENTS

# DATING A NIGHTMARE: AVOIDING, SURVIVING AND ESCAPING A COVERT NARCISSIST

# INTRODUCTION

COGNITIVE dissonance, I'm not sure why, but it's one of my favourite phrases. It just *sounds cool.* It sounds alien to me, and almost too intellectual to use in a normal sentence. You'd need to vet the person you're speaking with beforehand to ensure they'd know what it means when you say it. I once made the mistake of using the phrase 'Masochistic Equilibrium' in a sentence, and as the words came out of my mouth, I internally kicked myself for sounding pretentious. Only to my genuine surprise that the person knew what it meant.

"You know what masochistic equilibrium means?" I ask.

"Yes,"

"Masochistic. Equilibrium?" I reiterate, saying it slowly, unintentionally being more patronising.

"Yes!"

"Well, how about that?" I nod with a wry smile on my face, eyes glowing.

Back to it. Cognitive Dissonance, if for any reason you don't know what it means, humbly, I am happy to explain. It is when the person is incapable of accepting reality. Something has happened in their life, and it can be anything, but most likely a trauma, which has led that person to detach from reality. Their behaviour is inconsistent, their thought process does not match the reality and they are, for the most part, argumentative and stubborn for the sake of being argumentative and stubborn.

Have you ever met anyone who will just pick a fight with you? Regardless of if you're right or not, they'll just fight you? A classic example of cognitive dissonance, in a frivolous way, is spaghetti carbonara. "What?" you ask. Stay with me. This divides opinion (when it shouldn't), but spaghetti carbonara is not made with cream. There is no cream in a carbonara. You may put cream in it, and you may even call it a carbonara, you may even have been doing this for your whole life, but it still does not make it a carbonara. The 'creamy' sauce type of consistency in a carbonara is egg yolk and parmesan cheese, that's what gives it that texture. No cream.

As frivolous as this sounds, and it is, it is also a good example of a good chef, one who puts cream in their carbonara, fighting you to death for what they believe. They will not accept it. They can't accept the reality.

When it comes to psychology, we need to burrow further into the subconscious to fully understand cognitive dissonance as it is not simply a case of one being misinformed. Ignorance is one thing, refusing to accept the truth is another.

Let's just say a table is a table, and that's an example of an absolute and it's indisputable. Other examples are colours and numbers, for the most part, you can't really debate those too much, they are what they are.

Without digressing too much, a psychological bully will call you, for example, selfish, "You're selfish and you never help anyone." They could say this a million times over fifty years, but it doesn't make it true. To them that could be a truth, but what if you showed them years of noble behaviour? Hundreds of examples of times you've helped friends from tough situations, helped colleagues with their career, proactively improved someone's life, helped with a suicide attempt, given someone life changing advise, helped people with living arrangements or loaned people money? Would that person change their opinion of you? The answer is, no. They won't. They need to create a false 'truth'. Humans are not tables, we are not absolutes, unfortunately, we are subject to opinion, even if that opinion is about as researched and versed as a drugged-up pimp. Cognitive Dissonance is when someone's mind is incapable of seeing anything other than the 'truth' they have told themselves.

Recognise anyone like that?

You are most likely here because you have encountered a toxic relationship. You have perhaps at one time felt trapped and silenced. The toxic person in your life had refused to accept the truth and had tried to control the narrative. Painting you in ways you know you are not and anything you say or do is used against you. Oddly, sadly, their opinion will never change.

But guess what? They are mentally distressed, they are sad, they are depressed, and they are jealous of other people's happiness. What side do you want to be on? Happiness, of course.

They are also subject to 'truth' and gleefully I look forward to writing this book for you. There's a phrase, "never annoy an author," this is perhaps because when a toxic person tries to smear you, five or six people know, but when an author says something, it's carved in paper stone forever. This is a book narcissistic people do not want you to read.

Lives are ruined by the actions of a toxic spouse or partner. Through their own toxic mess, they pollute those around them. They try to control you, blackmail you, abuse you, lie about you, exploit you and all the while selling you and others a lie.

We will break it all down in this book and use examples of couples ranging from the beginning, from those still together heading toward the toxic end and those who are at the end picking up the remnants.

Cognitive Dissonance. It's sad in many ways in the sense that, people feel the need to detach from reality. The question has come up multiple times as to whether narcissism and toxic behaviour is innate or taught, but to me, and I'm happy to stand corrected on this, it's when someone has had a traumatic upbringing. The childhood is the foundation and if the child feels they have to build walls around them just to survive, then, right there they are living in a bubble, their own bubble. It's sad, it's definitely not good and as much as we want to express our frustrations to those who have done wrong to us, when taking a step back, it's best to view these people as chronically ill. So ill they will fall apart before our very eyes.

This book is called Dating A Nightmare simply because a nightmare can be determined as a very unpleasant and frightening experience. We can't always control whether they happen to us or not, however, we can control the sustained amount of time that nightmare is endured. We can all minimise the nightmares by seeing some of the red flags beforehand.

No one is a mind reader, we can never fully know what the future holds, nor can we ever fully understand other people. Even the staunchest body language experts will, at times, fall into certain traps. This isn't always because of lack of logic, it's because other emotions can overtake the rational thought process.

In Dating A Nightmare, I will highlight the red flags for you and lead you through the dark corridors of use cases and examples of toxic behaviour, narcissistic bullying, exploitation and psychological trauma you can look out for. We will dissect the key traits, the key red flags, the behaviour patterns and explore how one can overcome the situation. It's all about owning your thoughts, your happiness and doing what is in your control.

Remember, cognitive dissonance is a mental illness and some people will never accept there is no cream in a carbonara.

# CHAPTER 1
# A DEVIL IN PAUPERS CLOTHING

You meet your dream person. They seem great, charming, intelligent, spontaneous; they tick all of your boxes. Your life changes, you get those butterflies every time you think of their name, their smile, their face; you are, dare I say, in love with this person, and it's only been two dates!

This is the honeymoon stage, and, in truth, most relationships start out this way, it's the fun stage. However, with a narcissist, things are slightly different. They are your rock. They are the security you have always wanted, and this goes onto our first topic of Co-Dependency. The likelihood is, if you've dated or are dating a narcissist, you may have some co-dependency traits of your own to address.

Co-dependents need a dominant other to 'complete them', but not in a Jerry Maguire way, the needs of a co-dependent are acceptance. Somewhere in the co-dependent's life, they have not had the recognition or acceptance they have been looking for. This could be from a father or mother who showed little to no attention to them during childhood.

Starving someone of attention can go one of three ways; the person will propel themselves into something great, with an endless burning desire to always prove themselves. Often some of the world's most successful people have this trait. The other direction one could go in is self-destruction. The Giving-up approach where they fall into the traps of escapism. Drugs, party life, alcohol and anything they can do to escape the real world. Thirdly, one could go in another direction and adopt co-dependent traits whereby the traits of a 'superior' other boosts their own ego and self-confidence. In this situation, the co-dependent can fall into the trap of a narcissistic person, who controls the relationship, controls the agenda and controls the modus operandi. I believe the third option is the breeding ground for more narcissists. The co-dependent loses themselves and starts to act, speak, and think like the narcissist they have cuddled up to.

You don't have to answer which option you are, you may be parts of all three, that is very possible. Remember, humans are not absolutes, we are spiritual and ever evolving beings. However, it's important to understand what makes one co-dependent.

*  *  *

Let me introduce you to fictitious character number one, Jack. As a youngster, Jack felt isolated and alone. His dad worked all day and he barely seen him. When he did see his dad on weekends, he seemed disinterested and bothered by Jacks presence. This was normal for Jack. He never went on family holidays, never went on days out, never did 'fun' stuff. This was normal for Jack, how was he to know any different?

Jack forever wanted attention and acceptance. He wanted to be noticed. Like a cat who brings a captured mouse to the door for their owners to praise. If you starve someone of praise and encouragement, it can push them into one of the three paths we discussed earlier.

As a teenager, Jack was terrified of people and terrified of the opposite sex,

"Maybe they won't like me?" he would ask himself.

This is normal. If the family has never shown praise, encouragement or love, then how would Jack expect anyone else to offer those things? This made Jack become more reclused, more hidden and more introverted. He focused his time and energies into learning new skills and picked up a number of hobbies. He worked really hard and was determined to prove himself because innately, a little bit of encouragement and praise is all Jack is looking for.

Years pass like this and Jack is bullied by his family,

"I don't respect you,"

"You're useless,"

"You will never make it without us,"

"You're worthless."

Jack is lost. A toxic family will compound and fuel the flames of co-dependency. Remember, you are not these things being said of you, but doubt will creep in. Like an interrogation officer accusing you of something; over and over and over again, after many hours, trapped in a little white room in the corner on a steel chair, hungry and exhausted, perhaps you might start believing the accusations. This is gaslighting and it's a trait toxic people will use to paint their targets in certain ways. The key reason for this is they are insecure themselves. They are jealous and their bullying is sustained and disguised. Maybe they just hate you? That's possible, we have to accept family members can hate, through no reason other than jealousy, sexism and whatever else. It can happen.

Toxic family members love bullying, they love trampling on their targets' self-esteem, like a coven of witches.

"How dare you go off on your own without us,"

"How dare you try to be better than us."

That job promotion you got. Don't expect any praise. If they ask you how your day has been and you tell them, and if it's even remotely more interesting than theirs, expect a dirty look and a sigh of, "Oh here we go, he's bragging again." Toxic families are jealous to the core.

Toxic families want to make you dependent on them. For example, narcissistic parents, those who see themselves as God-Like and superior to others, will control you with money. Guess what, it's addictive! Money is good and easy money is even better. If it's there, it's hard not to go to it. In this toxic dynamic, everyone wins. The parent controls you and keeps you close; they are able to use the loaning of money as a manipulation tool down the line, and you get the extra pocket money and financial security that so many of us battle with daily.

Jack is insecure, bullied, trampled on and dependent on his family. He's trapped and he doesn't have the tools to fully survive on his own. He will, one day, but he needs to figure that out himself.

Now we have laid the foundation of Jack's past, let's see what adulthood could look like for him.

Jack has no luck with women, he can barely speak to them. As discussed, there is a history of childhood bullying and a lack of father figure, and this has created a root cause problem of low self-esteem and constantly questioning himself.

One day, a woman emerges from the smoke.

Jack is in awe. She is funny, attractive, charming, intelligent, beautiful. She ticks all the boxes.

This girl, we can call her Lucy, knows she is adored by men and possibly has multiple options available to her on any given day. Generally speaking, when entering a relationship with someone, it's important to establish, or at least understand, the relationship dynamic. Both sides are very rarely equal. In a relationship, usually one is more attractive, successful and in a position to boost the other financially, spiritually or psychologically. In this situation, Lucy is the superior. She knows she can do better than Jack, and she also knows she can manipulate him because he doesn't want to lose his newly found and unexpected catch.

This dynamic is not good for Jack. He is not in a position of emotional control because he will be pandering to Lucy's every need. She can cancel dates, make him pay for everything, subtly accuse him of not 'stepping up' to his side of things and she may not text him for hours per day, keeping him on edge. Meanwhile, Jack, already insecure about himself and whether Lucy likes him or not, is already out of control. Not in a negative way, but emotionally, his mind is over thinking and he is pandering and acting in accordance with the control of Lucy.

Lucy, in parallel, could be a narcissist who thrives on the control. That, we can never know, but she may be doing the same thing to multiple other people. Pulling and diverting attention and have people spiral out of control thinking of her.

***

Using the same relationship foundation, let's look at a different case study using the fictious character, Linda. Linda moves into

Matthew's home to start a relationship (and this can work across both genders). After three-four weeks, it becomes apparent Linda is not paying or contributing to any of the bills. Matthew comes home, the house is cold, the cupboards are bare, everywhere is a mess and Linda is laying in the bath in silence and in the dark.

They both go out for meals and Matthew pays for everything. The taxi trip to the restaurant, the coffee while on a shopping trip and everything in between. Linda is not contributing to anything. It's almost as if Linda sees herself as the self-entitled superior and Matthew must pay for everything in her life. Matthew notices quickly this is not an even relationship, in fact, Matthew's bills and outgoings have doubled with Linda being there.

Matthew then tries to bring up the conversation of a compromise but is quickly shot down.

"How dare you ask me to pay for bills?" she asks. Days later, it's possible Matthew's family call him, and the conversation could go something like,

"Did you ask Linda to pay rent?"

"No, I just brought up the conversation that maybe she should contribute to something in the house. She works and I'm finding it expensive to keep up her lifestyle. All the food, bills and even takeout costs are coming from me. She's not paying for anything!" Matthew protests.

"Well, she called us and told us you were trying to ask for rent from her," they inform.

"No, that's not the case," he protests.

Narcissistic and toxic people will try to manipulate their partners' family to turn them against their target in hope of trying to control the narrative. They are exploitative and try their best to get a 'free' life. Sadly, this opportunistic mentality doesn't serve much for them because they stay miserable.

Narcissists are not who they say they are. Initially, they will present themselves as meek, silent and nice. But the reality is, by saying less, they are hiding their true colours. Inside they are damaged to the core and it's only when they move into the home (like Linda did in our example), that the other person will start to see the true intentions of the toxic person.

Let's look back at our use case to see how other situations could work. Linda has moved herself into Matthew's home. But oddly, she has manipulated her way in. She had previously threatened Matthew with a number of things and blackmailed him into 'trying' it out. Only then, after she moved in, Matthew started to see and find out about the horrors of Linda's horrific and tortured past. Matthew also notices she'd passive aggressively bully him. Be careful of this, covert narcissists manifest their self misery by projecting onto others.

"Oh, that t-shirt looks a bit tight. Had enough chocolate?" they could say, or,

"Maybe you should skip dinner tonight," are a few example jibes. Narcissists subtly try to poke at your insecurities to destroy your happiness. Their jibes are not physical, narcissists very rarely have the physical power to overtly attack you, but they will covertly and subtly try to break you down. All the while, they themselves are the ones falling apart. When toxic narcissists are confronted with good, they will literally melt apart before your eyes. Shine good onto a toxic person and they won't know what to do, they will just wither.

Narcissists are extremely manipulative and look to draw on their guilt trip story for attention. They love playing the victim and getting sympathy from others, they feed off it. They are so good at playing the victim but will refuse to look introspectively at themselves (in a critical way). They will struggle to show empathy to others but not always by choice, they are just incapable of empathizing for others. This could lead to those around the narcissist to feel isolated, lonely and disregarded. The truth is, though this is the case, the narcissist is battling their own demons and for the most part are obsessed with themselves. If someone around the narcissist is suffering and in need of help, the narcissist won't be in a position to assist.

Covert narcissists hide in the shadows and do nothing to help others. All they care about is themselves. Using our case study, when Linda moves into Matthew's home, he notices the red flags early. She doesn't pay for anything, she spreads gossip to his family, she twists the truth to her friends and she is unwilling to listen to Matthew's thoughts or feelings. It's a constant web of lies, silence and deceit.

These are examples and I'm sure you will see similar patterns and behaviour in your situation. The patterns are predictable. Covert narcissists are the wolves in sheep's clothing which oddly might be offensive to the wolf. They are more akin to garbage with Burger King wrapping around it, what's inside is not nearly as appealing as the package suggests.

The covert narcissist sells a backstory to try to obtain emotional guilt and they use this to their advantage to manipulate. They see themselves as the victim so they can use that to leverage self-entitlement.

Unfortunately, it is often too late before you notice the toxic traits of a narcissist, they will have burrowed deep into your life before you truly find out about them. As the saying goes, when the mask slips and when you finally see the monster behind it, it will be too late.

In our case study, Linda is not contributing to anything in the house and is manipulating Matthew in multiple ways. She is not giving anything back to the relationship.

There will be no suggestions of fun. In fact, they are generally very plain and mundane people. By being this way, they are able to hide their true self. Being plain, quiet and mundane actually closes the door for any criticism. They are terrified of someone criticising them so they tend to remain quiet in social situations.

* * *

Toxic people will love bomb you. They do this because as they usually don't have any meaningful friends, they need you to be in their life, it's partly a survival mechanism. By Love Bombing you, it creates this illusion of how the relationship could be fun and it highlights the idea of building a life together. However, beware, it is just an agenda. You get caught up in the dream and fall for the spiel. It's only when you spend a week or two with these people that you find out how toxic, manipulative and lost they are.

Always do your due diligence before fully committing to someone. Humans are not absolutes, they are variable. We change, we shift, and we are many different personalities all at once. However, there are red flags to look out for before you fully commit so it's important to look out for the red flags.

Think carefully about taking the next step with a narcissist because if you go too far, it will get messy. Generally, it's not easy, but narcissists just suck the life out of you. They are not fun, they are not ambitious and everything they do is just desperate and feeble. If you're not getting genuine happiness and joy from your partner, then perhaps that's the key warning sign to step away.

If the goal of a relationship is for you to both love each other, boost each other up, co-exist and build an incredible life together, while also enjoying your life and helping each other. This cannot be achieved with a narcissist. It will be lopsided in their favour. In our two use cases, both Jack, Lucy, Matthew and Linda have somehow created an environment were the dynamic of the relationship is not equal, and it forces one of the personnel to constantly be compensating for an insecurity to keep the relationship afloat. The goal and the reality should be to build a loving partnership with trust, commitment, fun, passion and ambition.

## Summary

It's not easy identifying a toxic person or covert narcissist in the early stages of a relationship, but here are 10 traits to look out for –

1. They Never Say Sorry
2. Financially Exploit You
3. Blackmail & Threaten You
4. A Mundane, Plain personality
5. No Ideas for Fun (Travelling, Business Building, Excitement)
6. No real friends to speak of
7. Gossip about you to your family
8. Generally, just miserable to be around and suck the life out of you
9. Bully you with passive aggressive critical comments
10. Will Love Bomb you, selling you a perfect, fantastical relationship in the early stages

## Exercise

When did you realise the partner (or any toxic narcissist) in your life was not who they initially presented themselves to be?

_______________________________________

_______________________________________

_______________________________________

_______________________________________

_______________________________________

_______________________________________

_______________________________________

_______________________________________

_______________________________________

How did it make you feel?

_______________________________________

_______________________________________

_______________________________________

_______________________________________

_______________________________________

_______________________________________

_______________________________________

_______________________________________

## Notes

In this section, I'd like you to have a think about, brainstorm and write down a time in your life when you realised somebody's true colours. How did it make you feel and what will you be doing in the present and the future to react to the red flags?

__________________________________________________

__________________________________________________

__________________________________________________

__________________________________________________

__________________________________________________

__________________________________________________

__________________________________________________

__________________________________________________

__________________________________________________

__________________________________________________

__________________________________________________

__________________________________________________

__________________________________________________

__________________________________________________

__________________________________________________

__________________________________________________

__________________________________________________

__________________________________________________

# CHAPTER 2
## CO-DEPENDENCY
## AND THE ROYAL DYNAMIC

It's difficult to admit if you are co-dependent, but it is nothing to be ashamed of. If one has come from a troubled past were they have been starved of attention, love and encouragement, then that person could go down one of two paths. They could build walls around themselves and try to live a false life; essentially, becoming a narcissist. Or they could be fully dependent on someone 'superior' who can give them the life they want, all the while terrified of losing that support anchor and ending up alone.

The latter will force the co-dependent to sacrifice their own life and their own happiness to please the toxic superior. It's an example of the power dynamic in a relationship between a co-dependent and a narcissist.

It works across both genders. For example, let's use two characters to analyse a case study. Let's say Eva is in a weak position. She has no career path, she is lonely, is bitter at the world and is dependent on her family for income. She is struggling to find the right person to settle down with and has a history of dating younger guys with no future. Then, she, much like Jack, will not want to let someone go if they present themselves as the all-knowing, all successful oracle of life. This is a perfect breeding ground and opportunity for a narcissist to thrive. In this example, a narcissistic man, let's call him Kevin, could enter Eva's life with grand claims. Astronomical wealth, grand ambitions, a luxurious jet setting life and a troubled past (which pulls on the heart strings).

Narcissists are such great liars, they even convince themselves they are all of these things. Sadly, when you peel over the veil, there is nothing there. No investments, no business, no success story. Just a bogus backstory and a humble wage from a boss.

In this scenario, the person in the weak position will fall for the story and worship the narrative. The dynamic of the relationship is off to a terrible start. The lady in the weak position sees this new "Knight in shining armour" as her saviour. He can give her financial freedom, he can give her the holidays, he can give her an easy life which she was previously deprived of. Sadly, if there were troubles in the childhood, this man can also act as a new father figure for her.

Already we can see the power dynamic is wrong, and it creates an unstoppable chain of events. The narcissistic man loves the dynamic, he calls all the shots, he is the King of the castle and he is funding everything, therefore everyone must adhere to his rules. Perfect. For a narcissist this is exactly what they want. In turn, the weak lady will do anything to keep him happy. He is her saviour. She will pander to his every need and though they may argue from time to time, the narcissist can live his life, party and enjoy the fruits of his labour, while the co-dependent weak lady is unfortunately at home alone, and at the mercy of his every move and instruction. This example can work across both genders.

The power dynamic is an important red flag to look for and balance in this area is crucial for a healthy relationship. In reality, both parties should be contributing to the relationship in a spiritual and psychological way. Both should be benefiting the other person and helping each other to achieve their dreams. Like a team, a power couple were both sides are filling the downfalls of the other to make a formidable partnership.

Narcissistic people are self-entitled, they are not great believers of hard work and they would much prefer everything to be handed to them on a plate. Almost as if life owes them something.

The co-dependent, in this case, Eva, is dependent on Kevin for her existence now. She can't make it alone, so she defends him with her life. Any mention of Kevin being anything less than the maverick king he claims to be, will be met with loud animated rage and an overt (and fake) anxiety attack to gain sympathy. Sadly, this behaviour would be signs the co-dependent has become a narcissist themselves, submitting to the power dynamic and suppressing any sense of self. The Narcissist and the Co-dependent are both relying on a fake life to boost up the fake mirage of lies they have told themselves. Let's look at a few case study examples.

Eva and Kevin love grandeur. They see themselves as superior to others and will speak badly about others behind closed doors. They don't respect anyone. Eva and Kevin don't recognise other people's successes and will openly criticise other people's ambitions, hobbies and business ideas.

"That's not a real business," Kevin could spout, if someone in the family is trying to make some extra money with, let's say, piano tuition.

"From what I can see, that sounds like the behaviour of a little child," Kevin could say, if he and Eva want to falsely paint a person in a certain light.

They can't stand other people's success. So much so, they will make things up from thin air. Anything and everything they can think of will be used to undermine you. You could live hours away, but they will accuse you of "not helping out," when there is no example they can think of to justify the claim. A true leader, mentor and teacher will offer constructive feedback and offer an example. Narcissists can't do that. "You're a scumbag," they could say, but offer no example of why they think you are a scumbag. They happily brand people in certain ways because it allows them to continue their false grandeur when someone is deemed a threat to them. It is exhausting.

Eva and Kevin will never acknowledge or encourage someone. They are both from broken and troubled pasts and hand-to-glove are on a crusade of hate and criticism. They silently try to undermine others by simply not acknowledging certain people's existence and will never ask how someone is. That is an important red flag. Narcissists never ask how you are doing and what you have been up to. Their only goal is to extract information from you to criticise, not to encourage and not to start conversation.

Eva could have friends or family members who are far more intelligent and successful than her. Someone who has made a career for themselves and doing well in life. This will grate on the narcissist and they won't be able to accept it. Eva will do all she can to character assassinate that person to all those who will listen. All with the interest of making themselves feel better.

Eva is bitter at the world because deep down she knows she has sacrificed her life for a fake guru, but is now too far into the relationship she has become a narcissist herself.

That is the bad path a co-dependent can go down. The other path, as mentioned earlier in the chapter, is they can see the light.

They can accept their need for attention, love and emotional independence and from there can carve out a happy life for themselves.

* * *

Narcissists are a tower of cards, everything is fake with them. Their delusions of grandeur extend to their bizarre eating habits. This middle-class family, who, in the humblest possible way, may drive a hand-me-down Fiat in a moderate sized home, will brag about eating foie gras, gold leafed cheeseburgers and luxury quail eggs. They are quite literally in cuckoo world.

In parallel, they will never acknowledge anywhere you have been, achieved or seen. They don't care about anyone else, they just focus on their own house of cards and are doing everything they can to keep up appearances. The thought of anyone knowing they are living a hoax will terrify them and they cannot allow that to happen.

Narcissists will use every dirty trick in the book to suppress anyone who tries to oust them. Be wary of your credit report being cloned, your financial privacy being hacked and your private life being criticised constantly. They can do things like hack into your devices, stalk your social media and use their minions to write negative messages and ultimately, the objective is to embarrass you in some way. These are just a few examples of the things they can do. Be very prepared.

It is always about them, and they love to play the victim. Panic attacks are common with narcissists as this is a physical type of attention seeking. They love to stir up negative energy and play the role of the ultimate misunderstood victim. It also stems from the idea that narcissists are not particularly good at expressing their feelings. What a narcissist projects to the world is, for the most, is a lie. Their true feeling and energy is boiling up inside them until they manifest an attack on themselves when their body literally starts to spiral out of control.

As mentioned, they are living a fake life and are in cuckoo world. There is no investments to speak of, no business to show, no history of success, no recognised money, no happy past, it's just this mirage of talk with the hope of duping anyone who will listen.

Narcissists don't like your success or happiness. That new car you saved up to buy, that new house you've bought, that new promotion you've got in work, they won't acknowledge it. Why? Because they don't have those things. All they have to talk about is their quail eggs and gold leaf cheeseburgers. Fake people. Fake life.

* * *

Bringing this full circle, if you think you are a co-dependent, you really do need to break away from it. It's possible not to be trapped in the claws of a narcissist. What will end up happening is you will keep trying to make the narcissist happy and they will feed off the attention. Beware, it will never end, deep down, they will never be satisfied. Narcissists are only happy and satisfied when others are suppressed and miserable, just like them. They always want to feel like they are the winners, the ones in control and the ones doing better than everyone else.

Narcissists are spineless enough to covertly attack, but then hide in the shadows and twist it if you call them out on it. They will accuse their targets of hiding, but in truth, it is them who are hiding. Narcissists use flying monkey's to defend themselves, protect their name, and protect their reputation. Often, this could be the co-dependent doing this. They refuse to accept feedback or criticism for something someone sees as wrong.

Being in a narcissistic relationship is imbalanced because the target is pandering to the narcissists every need. The narcissist is prone to self-destruction and it is common for the narcissist to self-harm in some way. This could be through isolation, monetary recklessness or perhaps a gambling, drug or alcohol addiction.

Narcissists can't admit weakness, they believe themselves to be perfect and will not entertain the idea of seeking advice from anyone. They truly believe they are the king or queen of their make-believe world. So, when it comes to something like addiction, it's important to understand some of the key traits to look out for and why a narcissist may steer towards self-destructive behaviour.

## Denial

Narcissists will never accept the true reality of their lives and their whole existence is a web of deceit, lies and falsities. A narcissist will never accept they are anything less than perfect, and anything that potentially damages that delusion will be quickly dismissed.

## Refusal to take Responsibility

Narcissists will blame others for their mishaps. Nothing is ever their fault. They can never apologise, will struggle to lift others up and believe the world owes them something, simply for them existing and being the "awesome people they are."

## Self-Destructive

Narcissists are tortured inside. They have a lot of demons, which plays into their hands when seeking attention from a loving co-dependent. They will spin this story and the co-dependent will confuse a childhood of trauma with success. Simply by "going through a lot," this person's success level and credibility will shoot up. Don't fall for the trap. These tales of trauma are designed to sucker you in, and they feed off the sympathy. It can also be used as a tool to manipulate you down the line. Narcissists are always escaping. They need to escape because deep down, they are living a lie and the burning inferno inside them will never stop. They are incurable beings forever trapped in a lie.

## Others will Suffer

Anyone around the narcissist will themselves feel lonely and abandoned. The Narcissist is too selfish to think of his or her partner and will continue to live their life exactly how they want. They may party a lot, refuse to spend time with their partner and they will only want to do things when it fits them. It is common for the partner of a narcissist to feel completely unloved and rejected while the narcissist seemingly continues to live a double life.

## Controlling

The narcissist loves to control their environment so using drugs or alcohol is a way to do this. Others will suffer when their personality changes instantly from happy to rage to whatever else, constantly keeping their partner on edge. Remember what we said earlier, the relationship is imbalanced heavily to the side of the narcissist.

## <u>Superficial</u>

Any relationship with the narcissist is superficial. Expect inappropriate public displays of affection, public touching, constantly calling each other "babe," in public. Just think of the most cringe worthy superficial relationship, then that is most likely a narcissistic couple. Superficial, they want to be the richest, most successful and fairest of them all.

## <u>Shame</u>

Narcissists are self-involved, all they think about is themselves. Furthermore, they hate themselves. There is a feeling of shame deep within them which they are constantly trying to escape from. This is where an addiction, like drugs or gambling could come into the fold. They will seek a lot of attention from prostitutes or other people. They need love, they need attention (negative or positive) and they are happy to keep stirring the pot. Narcissists are like a rabid animal finding blood to get that attention.

For the most part, narcissists are plain, mundane and don't really have any friends. Often the co-dependent and the narcissist are a troublesome duo, both miserable but both benefiting each other. The narcissist gets their supply of praise, love and king-like admiration, while the co-dependent has financial security and a dominant father figure in their life, propping up their wafer thin self-esteem which is one puff away from blowing to dust.

* * *

The other path a co-dependent can go is full independence. Why live a fake life? Say no to being cheated on. Say no to being lied to.

Say no to being exploited. Say no to being in a relationship which is not equal. As mentioned earlier, the superiority dynamic is shifted in these relationships and it is not equal. You will be drained of your independence, your joy and you will be constantly in a spiral of a) maintaining a fake life, b) not being respected, c) having no life goals and d) constantly questioning the secret life of your narcissistic partner.

It's possible for a co-dependent to rise up again. They can be proud of who they are and build their own business, have their own hobbies and have their own friends. It's possible for a co-dependent to live a life where it's not built on criticising others.

Narcissists see themselves as the beacon of morality, everyone should live and be exactly how they think. However, they themselves are not a good example of this. Their life, for the most part, is mediocre. They have a grandeur problem. They will brag about how big their house is, how amazing their life is and how much great stuff they have, but in reality, there is nothing there.

Narcissists are innately jealous and have zero regard for other people's existence.

The irony is, they love attention, so if a narcissist reads this and it fits in with who they might be, they will actually enjoy it. Narcissists and toxic people love that they get under people's skin and love notoriety, even if it is negative.

## Summary

Being a co-dependent is not a crime but it can become troublesome if you don't act on the key behavioural patterns. Here are 13 red flags and traits to look out for if you think you are co-dependent and/or with a narcissist.

1. Constantly seeks approval from others
2. Needs to be surrounded by successful people all the time
3. Brags about the things they eat
4. Never encourages anyone and never says "well done" to people
5. Never asks how other people are doing
6. No business or success story to speak of
7. Have to constantly posture about how great their life is
8. Miserable, always questioning what their partner is up to
9. Secretly knows their partner is cheating, but refusing to act upon it to keep up appearances
10. Being hyper critical of any constructive feedback
11. Having zero interest in other people's lives
12. Always feeling underappreciated and undervalued

## **Exercise**

What are the key traits of a co-dependent and an empath?

_______________________________________________

_______________________________________________

_______________________________________________

_______________________________________________

_______________________________________________

_______________________________________________

_______________________________________________

_______________________________________________

_______________________________________________

_______________________________________________

Are you a co-dependent or an empath? If so, what character traits do you possess?

_______________________________________________

_______________________________________________

_______________________________________________

_______________________________________________

_______________________________________________

_______________________________________________

_______________________________________________

_______________________________________________

_______________________________________________

_______________________________________________

## Notes

In this section, write down your thoughts on the dangers of being a co-dependent and write down an example in your life of when this scenario has played out.

# CHAPTER 3
# A TORTURED PAST

Covert Narcissists are classic examples of people who use their tortured past for sympathy. Sympathy and attention to a narcissist is a manipulation tool and fuel for their broken ego. Like a vampire to blood, sympathy, attention and being doted on is energy to them, commonly known as Narcissistic Supply. Though these things are important for healthy individuals, covert narcissists need this supply constantly, they depend on it.

In parallel to this, narcissists use their past as a way to manipulate the people around them. Empaths or co-dependents will dose the narcissist with unlimited amounts of sympathy and love, solely because of their troubled past. The narcissist, in turn, will want more and more of this and will use this 'supply' for their own ego.

As mentioned in the previous chapter, if you are a co-dependent (or an empath), you need to make sure you are not fueling the wrong persons ego. Make sure your love is balanced, in moderation and ensure to not give a potential narcissist provisions to act and behave a certain way because of their past.

Let's look at our use case of Linda and Matthew and see how this can reveal itself in real life ways.

Linda kept her past secret from Matthew, until she had burrowed into his life and established her opportunistic self into his existence. Linda, the covert narcissist, has Matthew exactly where she wants him when she gets close to him.

As time goes on, Matthew starts to learn disturbing things about Linda. Some examples of this could be as extreme and disturbing as having sexual relations with another family member, a history of drug and alcohol addiction or chronic disguised mental illness. Matthew wouldn't have known these things earlier, but it would be too late for him to back out as covert narcissists are opportunistic and will remain plain and meek until they have snuck their way into someone else's life.

The very definition of covert is it is disguised. It is slow and methodical. What appears to be harmless will be the thing which wants to extract as much pain, attention and suffering from you as possible.

This stems from a past starved of attention and narcissists crave this relentlessly. Be wary of how they treat pets, especially if that pet gets more attention than them. Matthew could notice how Linda would treat the family dog, feeding it chocolate to almost kill it, letting it escape on purpose or dehydrating it to within an inch of it's life. Be very careful of your pets around these type of people. They lack empathy and are unable to show love and compassion to other things, all they want to do is extract, consume and take from others.

If you show your pet love and affection (as you should), expect extreme jealousy from the narcissist and expect the animal to be harmed in some way by the jealous narcissist.

Covert narcissists most likely have a troubled past, but also they refuse to get help. They have extreme abandonment issues and they don't take rejection very well. Breaking up with a narcissist is not a normal situation and some of the things you can expect from them are as follows:-

1.   They become vindictive
2.   Shocked at the rejection and will try to attack you
3.   Will try and try to turn others against you
4.   Unable to move on
5.   Unable to apologise and see their mistakes
6.   Will stalk your social media
7.   Refuse to resolve conflict

It's important to note that the seeds of toxic are sown early on in life. They may build walls around themselves as a defense mechanism to hide their true identity but at the same time fuel themselves with their toxic past. Healthy people will recognize these patterns and will seek help, while toxic people remain in denial, leading to their behaviour having a negative knock-on effect on the people around them.

* * *

Narcissists can go to counselling, but they will most likely not continue the sessions. They want to wallow in their misery as this is what is comforting to them. It's often known as the masochistic equilibrium and trauma bonding. The toxic person associates themselves with the misery, and actually uses it as an excuse for a) sympathy (to get seemingly endless supply for their ego), b) to treat people badly (they blame it on their stress levels), c) to be mothered and fathered (they expect everything to be spoon fed to them and d) they use it as an excuse to not work and free load off other people.

They don't want help because their misery is part of the fabrics of who they are.

Narcissists use their backstory to trap co-dependents and empaths. The latter will love someone more if they are troubled because they feel they can fix them. If you are an empath, don't try to fix people. You may have encountered someone who does not want to be fixed. Co-dependents specifically hold people with troubled pasts in high regard, almost as if their circumstances have made a 'warrior' of that person and made them superior to everyone else.

* * *

Let's use one of our use cases to dig into a few examples. Jack and Lucy have been together for a few years, as established, the power dynamic is shifted in Lucy's favour, but the relationship has survived because Jack is doing everything he can not to lose his "out-of-his-league" new girlfriend. Lucy tells Jack how she had a troubled past, her parents left her early and she was raised by a long-lost uncle. Jack loves her more. He rationalises her current behaviour of being stand-offish, rude, cold and manipulative with her troubled past story. Jack starts to *understand* why all of this is happening and he continues to stick with it. It's just a trap. Lucy is refusing to get help for her own problems and is using it as an excuse to treat Jack poorly and manipulate him. In a twisting cycle, Jack is being emotionally manipulated.

This is a classic example of how domestic abuse works. The abuser will often blame a troubled past, an external source or *something else* for the psychological or sometimes physical abuse they are inflicting on their partner. Remember, this can work for both males and females. Both genders can be abusers.

Jack starts to hold Lucy in higher regard, and she starts to get away with more and more abuse. She shouts at him, hits him at times and tells him he has to be home by a certain time. It's all very chaotic, but Lucy will mix this in with overt acts of love and affection, which Jack is craving and then he forgets the previous acts of anger and bullying he has experienced.

These examples are designed to help you identify how a narcissist and a co-dependent can fuel each other, if they both don't seek help and if they both try to obtain from the other the thing they are craving (which can never be fulfilled). It is an endless cycle of trauma for both sides.

* * *

Narcissists use their troubled past to be the king or queen of their universe. They become control freaks. This is because when they were younger, they didn't have control, it was taken away from them. Therefore, their whole life, for the most part, is a fabricated discrete world where they live in their 'castle' and all of the people in it *are their peasants.* This will also be the same for the co-dependent if they are complicit with the narcissist.

If you suspect you may be dating a narcissistic person, look for the red flags and specifically zone in on their childhood. If it is troubled, then that is an important starting point. People can't change their past, of course, most people have had issues in the past. That is not the crime. The issue is when the narcissist refuses to get help and refuses to acknowledge the impact of their childhood. Facing the problem head on is the best way, as opposed to creating a fake life and fake self-projection which negatively impacts the people around them.

* * *

Let's look at a case study example, to see another way childhood trauma could impact someone's life in adulthood. Eva and Kevin are a happy couple, but Kevin is hellbent on telling Eva, his friends (the few that he has) and anyone who cares to listen of how rich he is. He will happily tell them how much money he made last month, and he will constantly talk about money. This is not normal behaviour. Kevin has linked financial wealth with self-worth and is making the unhealthy link in his own mind. What Kevin also thinks is that other people link self-worth with financial prosperity and feels he needs to live up to that.

Kevin will make grand claims about parties he will be throwing, houses he will be buying, famous people he knows, food he's eaten and places he has been as a way to boost his self-worth and impress others. These are all false, but you will find it is always *something* being mentioned. Some grand claim that will soon be coming to fruition, but it never does.

Something the famous magician and illusionist Derren Brown once said,

"Extraordinary claims, require extraordinary evidence."

Derren wasn't talking about narcissism when he said that, but the phrase can be used as an example. Sometimes, it's best not to brag. Trying to boast about your life serves minimal purpose and for the most part, will just cause resentment and well, people will think you are pompous. No one likes pompous.

If we use a real-life example, though somewhat extreme, Ted Bundy was someone who had a troubled past. I have a problem with society almost celebrating the lives of these monsters and I don't think there is anything too fascinating about someone who does something to end up in jail. However, one of the areas of Bundy's childhood, which doesn't get mentioned much, is how his mother had lied to him and it was his sister who pretended to be his mother.

When linking such an act of mistrust and betrayal from the women in his life in his childhood to the actions he chose to undertake in adulthood, it's easy to see how he'd have such an innate hatred toward women. This is a crude and extreme example, but hopefully showcases how a troubled past can be the root cause for physical and psychological offenses in adulthood.

In summary, if someone is constantly bragging and discussing their riches, take it as a red flag. People who are not mentally ill don't need to link their self-worth to financial prosperity, they simply just need to show up. Down to earth people can be ambitious without overtly shouting about it. The narcissists will be triggered by your happiness, confidence and success, and though they won't mention anything about your life to you, they are secretly stalking and watching your every move. It is triggering them. They can't stand the sight of you being happy and successful.

## **Summary**

Here is a list of red flags to look out for in relation to a narcissist and their troubled past –

1. Discusses their troubled past in detail, playing the victim
2. Mentions their past a lot to obtain attention, more love and sympathy
3. Has a past of being with a lot of sexual partners (those with troubled pasts have issues connecting with others and will either have lots of sexual relations and/or will cheat on their partners)
4. Acts as if they are the King or Queen of their world
5. Will make grand claims about their life and projects that are forthcoming (which never materialise)
6. Will talk about money and will find any way to mention how "wealthy" and "great" they are (they are linking their self-worth to financial prosperity)
7. They hate a particular gender or type of person (They may overtly hate men, women or a particular type of person and will be vocal about it – both men and women do this)
8. They make excuses for their rude behaviour, using their past to justify it
9. They don't want to get help and are married to their troubled and toxic past

## **Exercise**

What tortured past story did the narcissist in your life share with you?

How did the narcissist use this story against you in your relationship?

# Notes

In this section, write down your thoughts on this hypothesis and how you feel a tortured past will result in the creation of a narcissist.

# CHAPTER 4
# THE NARCISSISTIC COUPLE

You have most likely picked up this book because at some point in your life, most likely in the recent past or present, have been in contact with someone you suspect to be a narcissist. Though we have focused mostly on how you yourself can avoid these type of people, it's also important to highlight some of the traits to observe in a narcissistic couple, so either a) you can avoid them and b) ensure you don't fall into the trap of becoming superficial and toxic like them.

## <u>Delusions of Grandeur</u>

Narcissists love to boast about what they are doing, what they have been doing and where they will be going. Expect major projects, building plans, exciting business ideas and the most luxurious restaurants to be part of their conversation. They will gloat about the things they have, the size of their tv or the size of their house. "Things" are very important to the narcissist. They use material things as a way to boost their own confidence and showcase a luxurious existence to others.

## <u>Jealousy</u>

Expect extreme jealousy from a narcissistic couple, and, as comical as it sounds, they exhibit copycat behaviour. If you go sky diving, they will go sky diving. If you play a musical instrument, they will play a musical instrument. If you play a particular sport, they will play a particular sport. They always want to one-up others. However, interestingly, they are the only ones playing that game. Healthy, ambitious and self-driven people are doing these things because they find enjoyment from them, it's a passion of theirs and it brings meaning to their life. The narcissist is only doing it because they want to be the best at everything. They can't handle the idea of someone being happy and more talented, and God forbid, richer than them.

## Critical

They are hyper critical of others. When you think of leaders; they have a warmth to them that encourage others, are approachable and they want to lift others up. That's the sign of a great leader. Narcissists are the opposite to that, they are only critical of others, they only want to crap on people and want others to be unhappy. If someone tries to start up a business, expect this to be mocked. No words of encouragement, no warm words of advice, just critical comments to make you second guess yourself and lower your self-esteem. Why do they do this? This goes back to point 2, they are jealous. They don't have the drive and determination of healthy people. They just sit back in their house of cards, in their fake life, worrying what the world thinks of them. Sadly for them, it quickly becomes obvious to the people around them what type of person they are.

## Bullies

This is an extension of the previous point, but you guessed it, they are bullies! They are quick to smear others and are happy to vocalise this to anyone who will listen. A narcissist will ignore you, but then cry to others that it was you who ignored them, they love playing the victim to their minions. Spinning a sob story and twisting the narrative to make themselves the victim is exactly what the narcissist loves to do.

## Poor Communicators

Narcissists will not speak to you face to face. This is partly because they see themselves as above people. The Queen wouldn't speak to a peasant, will she? They refuse to speak to people whom they don't perceive to be on their majestic level. This will fuel negative thoughts and feelings. An Empath is kryptonite to a narcissistic couple because he or she will know everything about them and see right through their BS with just one look. The empath really does have that superpower to infiltrate the veil of illusion the narcissist likes to project. Therefore, if you are an empath, don't expect the narcissist to want to speak to you too much, you are the eagle to their rat. They are terrified of you!

## Promiscuous

Narcissists are promiscuous and are prone to infidelity. This is just theoretical, but when we add up the behaviour patterns, it seems to add up to that. Let's break it down.

- They are selfish. They only think about themselves.
- They love attention and will do anything and everything to get it from anyone who will give it.
- Self-destructive. They are naturally sociopathic and will do things they know are wrong. The likelihood is, cheating on their partner is an exciting thing for them.

- Reckless with money. They believe themselves to be millionaires and will go bankrupt trying to prove it to themselves and others. A night out at the strip club or brothel bar is probably not out of the question for a narcissist.

- They need love. I know I mentioned they need attention in this list, but it needs to be added again. They need attention and this is an endless well of need for them. If given the opportunity, how could they resist the charms of a seductive vixen?

Finally, narcissistic couples are losers. Apologies for the blunt phrasing, but it's really true. Let's break down a few traits of a loser, and you decide if it fits in with the suspected narcissist in your life.

**Traits of a Loser**

## Gossip and Smearing others

They love to gossip about others and try to tear people down. Very rarely will they have the integrity or self confidence to say it to your face. Nor will they want to give you constructive feedback. They will just talk about you behind your back, and cleverly say just enough for you to find out about it. They are passive aggressive bullies, and this is what makes them losers.

## Pessimistic

They are always pessimistic. If you tell them a business idea or something you plan to do, put your last dollar on the idea being scrutinised, criticised and slammed to such a degree you'll be put off even wanting to do it. Narcissists believe they are the only ones capable of doing anything and everyone else is useless. This type of contempt and lack of respect to others makes them a loser.

## Lack Empathy

Narcissists lack empathy. They are unable to feel for another man or woman. This is because they see everyone else as their enemy. Quite simply, they are Machiavellian and want to conquer everything and everyone. By you even existing, you are an enemy to them. Narcissists lack compassion to their enemies. This is acceptable in a competitive situation, but narcissists see everyone as an opponent and everyone as a threat. This makes them a loser.

## No Ambition

Narcissists lack ambition. They just want to copy others and try to one-up them. They themselves believe to be perfect and the peak of human capability. In truth, they lack real passions and nothing makes them happy apart from crapping on others and defeating others; that's what makes them happy. It's all they seem to live for, defeating others and self-indulgence.

## No Respect

How can they respect anyone when they don't even respect themselves? They hate themselves! Therefore, unfortunately, they will never respect you. Or anything for that matter. They will say comments like, "respect is earnt," sure, but a minimal level of respect is owed to good people of the world who are trying their best. The level of respect can increase if somebody does extraordinary things, but I truly believe, unless the person is a murderer, rapist or just a deplorable who lacks ambition and class, then a certain level of human respect is owed to that person. We are all in this mess together and we need to help each other where we can. Narcissists aren't like this, they won't respect you, and they will never give you that respect. This makes them an extraordinary loser.

## **Quitters**

Narcissists seem themselves as royalty, so they don't really believe in hard work. You know, really fighting for something they want? They don't believe in working hard to reach a milestone that brings them a step closer to their dream situation. They just believe they are entitled to everything and they are fueled by competing with others, not by passion. Therefore, most things these people start, ends in a few months. They are quitters. They don't know hard work, they don't know teamwork, they don't know ambition, all they know is how to be pessimistic self-hating jealous copycats. This makes them a loser.

## **Closed Minded**

Narcissists are not open-minded people. They believe everyone should do as they do and listen to everything they do. Everyone else is beneath them. They are mean spirited people who talk bad about others. This makes them closed minded, and bonified losers.

## Summary

Here is a list of red flags to look for if you suspect you are in the midst of a narcissistic couple –

1. Delusions of Grandeur
2. Jealous
3. Critical of others
4. Bullies
5. Mean spirited
6. Poor communicators
7. Promiscuous
8. Pessimistic
9. Lack Empathy
10. No real ambition that stems from passion
11. Inability to respect others

## **Exercise**

What traits have you seen in your suspected narcissistic couple?
What did they do and how did they behave?

___________________________________________________

___________________________________________________

___________________________________________________

___________________________________________________

___________________________________________________

___________________________________________________

___________________________________________________

___________________________________________________

___________________________________________________

___________________________________________________

How does the Narcissistic couple react to criticism?

___________________________________________________

___________________________________________________

___________________________________________________

___________________________________________________

___________________________________________________

___________________________________________________

___________________________________________________

___________________________________________________

___________________________________________________

## **Notes**

In this section, write down your thoughts on narcissistic couples and any traits mentioned in this chapter that ring true for you, as well as any other ideas that can be incorporated into the study.

_______________________________________________

_______________________________________________

_______________________________________________

_______________________________________________

_______________________________________________

_______________________________________________

_______________________________________________

_______________________________________________

_______________________________________________

_______________________________________________

_______________________________________________

_______________________________________________

_______________________________________________

_______________________________________________

_______________________________________________

_______________________________________________

_______________________________________________

_______________________________________________

_______________________________________________

_______________________________________________

_______________________________________________

# CHAPTER 5
# THE BURNING BRIDGE:
# THE INEVITABLE END

Breaking up with a narcissist is not your standard break up. Nothing is normal about cutting ties and ending a relationship with a toxic person. To dissect this, first we need to reiterate some of the key traits of the narcissist.

**Self-Entitled.** They see themselves as being above others. They will shop at luxurious places, eat luxurious foods and hold a moral high ground above almost everyone they encounter. They simply believe they are perfect, everyone must and should love them and they must always get what they want. When these points break down, when *your heinous* is disobeyed or feels disrespected then expect the *Wicked Witch of The West* to emerge from their meek shadow.

**Controlling**. They love to control their environment and the people in it. They don't really have friends, it'd be hard to count one good friend of theirs they can call and seek advice from. They show a facade, even to their friends. No one knows the real them. Perhaps even they themselves don't know who their real self is. If you question anything, expect the Shakespeare-like public breakdown and dramatics. If they feel like they are losing control and forced into circumstances they didn't plan for, then expect the teeth of a ravenous spineless wolf to sink into you.

**Lonely and Tormented.** Sadly, they do have a tortured past with lots of abandonment issues. In a twisted way, they are a victim also, just they step into the dark side when they try to torment others and bring others down to their depressing and self-loathing level. Abandonment to a toxic narcissist is a major blow to their ego and already low self-esteem. Often, the narcissist will break up with you first, to avoid having the displeasure of accepting someone didn't want them. In the same instance, narcissists can't be alone as the attention and admiration from others is what keeps their ego and self-esteem propped up. Breaking up with a narcissist will bring those feelings of torment, abandonment and loneliness back for them. As a result, expect pure rage and fury to be thrown at you.

When you mx in self entitlement, delusions of grandeur, controlling behaviour and a tormented past, you have the destructive combination for chaos and disaster. There is no easy way to say this, but expect your life to get very messy, very quickly.

* * *

Now that we have laid the groundwork for the type of person you may be dealing with. Let's look at some of the things that may be happening before the breakup.

They do not listen. Narcissists do not care for a single word you say, only if it is critical of them, then they will plot to get revenge on you, not actually acknowledge the feedback. This will inevitably put strain on a relationship. How can a relationship survive when one side simply does not acknowledge a single word the other says? Of course, the narcissist will twist this and will project your feedback onto you. If you tell them they don't listen, they will say the same about you. If you tell them they are too sensitive or angry, they will reply by accusing you of the same. They are incapable of taking any type of criticism.

This could be for many reasons, but it may be because you are a threat to them. Narcissists, in their quest for survival and innate desperation to preserve their reputation and self-esteem, see the world as somewhat of a jungle. You are the Lion to them, the superior, righteous, successful dominant one who they aspire to be. Rather than team up with you or learn from you, they want to passive aggressively condemn you. They disregard your successes, they won't support you, they'll never ask how you are, they don't want to know anything about you, only what they hear through rumour. Essentially, anything good that you do, they will bury their head in the sand.

In parallel to not listening to you, you will see the relationship as imbalanced. They are exploitative people. All they want from you is money. They are consumers. They take, but they don't give. You can't grow with someone like this. If a healthy relationship is built on a fortress of equality, were both sides help each other to grow, support each other, contribute to bills, have fun coliving and generally being there for each other, then a narcissistic relationship can be perceived as the opposite to that.

The longer the relationship goes on, the more you will see behind the mask of the person they were portraying themselves to be, you will uncover their dark and ugly side, which is more horrifying than anyone could imagine. As mentioned previously, they will act like the innocent cute gremlin, but inside they are the demonic spawn from the same movie.

They are incredibly controlling and one of the reasons you may wish to end things with a narcissist is because they want to manage your full schedule. If you go out and have fun without them, expect immense jealousy and revenge. They won't want you go to the bars after work and they won't want you to have an independent life. They will use extreme measures of emotional guilt tripping and control to ensure you lose all of your independence. They want you to do exactly as they say. Remember, they want to control their environment and the people in it.

* * *

After you've finally decided to break up with the narcissist. Expect to be threatened. They will threaten you with legal action, financial exploitation, taking your children away, moving far away. They will threaten these things and use blackmail tactics to keep their targets close. They see themselves as worthless and the only way they feel they can keep their targets close is by using threatening and blackmailing behaviour.

They may even change slightly and start putting on the act again to convince you they've changed, only to eventually go back to the demonic monster they revealed shortly after burrowing into your life. You are simply a commodity to them, someone to give them a free life, they don't listen, they will take, they will cheat, and they will blackmail you to keep you close.

Even after all of this, if you muster the courage to leave, expect an onslaught of narcissistic rage to come your way. Let's break down some of the areas they will go after.

<u>**Financial**</u>

They will try to attack you financially and will look to not only bankrupt you, but to also extract as much money from you as possible. This will be a painful experience for you, but don't worry. It will be temporary and there is always a way out. You can use it as motivation to generate more income streams and build your businesses. Simply by someone robbing money from you, it could be the push you need to go for that promotion or go for that investment you've been meaning to do. As the saying goes, try to turn lemons into lemonade.

<u>**Children**</u>

Expect a vicious battle for your kids. The narcissist doesn't want to meet you in the middle on anything when it comes to children. Their grandeur delusion is too deep rooted and they are terrified of their child hearing the truth, which will put the narcissist in a negative light. In addition, they see themselves as royalty so believe the child should be raised by their standards, not by yours.

A narcissist will never want to write a deal down. You could record a conversation and they will still deny it, unless it is in writing, they will not commit. They are the ultimate control freaks.

Let's discuss a few ideas during a custody battle. Before we dive in, please note this book is not in any way formal legal advice, please do seek help and guidance from a professional. In the spirit of exploring ideas, let's look at the following.

Don't say or do anything that will incriminate you. Expect the goal posts to keep on moving when it comes to the narcissist. They want disruption, they want to be the puppet master and they will do everything to keep you from seeing your children. Partly, this is because they may be operating under shame and are petrified of their child finding the truth about what they did. They want to manage their reputation at all costs. In parallel, they will enjoy the destructive attention. The misery this will cause you will bring them happiness. They want you to suffer.

Though the narcissist will want to financially exploit you, and rip you from your children, they will of course deny all of this and will continue to maintain a particular image to the people close to them. For example, they will refuse to answer the phone, refuse to work on an arrangement, refuse to communicate with you, but if you block your telephone number as a reaction to the constant manipulation, they will tell all of their friends that "you are blocking communication." Completely disregarding the years of broken arrangements, lies, manipulation and blocked access from their side. They just pick on your reaction and use that for their victim story. It's all about their reputation guarding. A narcissist can never admit fault and is obsessed with how people perceive them.

During the relationship, you can be perfect. Never home late, pay all the bills, never home drunk, take your partner out for meals and treat them well, but after a breakup, a narcissist will find anything to attack you and smear your name. Even if it resorts to fabricating stories.

## Sabotage

A narcissist will stalk you relentlessly. Every social media page you may have will be frequently visited. Beware of this and don't post anything that will incriminate you. They are waiting for you to say and do something that they can use against you. It's a violent desperation to try everything to hurt you. And once they hurt you, guess what? They will keep hurting you, over and over again. By you breaking up with them, they don't have the coping mechanism or self-esteem to accept it, so they want to strike out. Their anger is channeled into getting revenge on you.

Block anyone who is not a close friend or trusted. Don't accept friend requests from people you don't know, beware of 'flying monkeys'. For those of you new to the topic, 'flying monkeys' are people around the narcissist who are stalking you on behalf of the narcissist. They are trying to gather information on you to use against you. It is a relentless attack and it is never ending.

Download anti-virus software for your phone and handset devices. Do research on how you can keep your technology and privacy settings safe. They will try to hack into your phone and read all of your messages and view all of your photos. Don't open unknown links and don't open any untrusted or unknown attachments. They are trying to attack you.

Don't post anything happy on your public social media pages. This sounds bizarre, but your happiness is a direct attack to the narcissist and their eyes will glow with rage and they will come for you. They will find more ways to attack you. Post happy photos, but just on your personal pages with trusted people on it. Happiness will lead to more revenge from them, they will contact law enforcement and make up more lies to try to disrupt your life.

In parallel to this, narcissists will use anything and everything against you and will even twist events to justify their attacks. As mentioned earlier, they will not answer your calls, but then blame you for blocking your number. It's all about control. They want to constantly manipulate the situation and when you regain control they will try to blame you for it.

They will provoke you, prod you and bully you, but when you react, they will run, cry and moan to anyone who will listen, mostly to their minions. They will try to obtain as much sympathy as possible while branding *you* as the bully. They love drama and they can't understand how their actions and behaviour can be provocative. They will look for you to react so they can then pin blame on you.

## <u>Word Salad</u>

A narcissists whole objective is to confuse the situation and often their rhetoric is confusing, contradictory and moving from A to Z without the appropriate bridging. Why? Because they are either trying to conceal their true intentions to keep up their "perfect" appearance or they are purposely looking to disrupt the conversation, which in turn is a control mechanism. It could also mean they are doing everything they can to conceal themselves through the confusion. Let's use one of our cases studies as an example of how this could look.

Kevin and Lucy are in a custody battle for their two-year-old child. Lucy informs she wants the child to see Kevin frequently, but when asked when that can be arranged, she back pedals and says she doesn't know. Later in the conversation, Lucy will backtrack from her objective, and will say she doesn't trust Kevin. Then when asked why she doesn't trust, she will answer something unsubstantiated like,

"He may say bad things about me to him." The narcissist only cares about their reputation and how they are being perceived, so they will try to protect this "perfect" appearance in any way they can. If the toothpaste leaves the tube, there's no turning back for a narcissist. They are terrified of people knowing the real them.

Other ways narcissists will try to confuse proceedings is, they will state an opinion or request and then when it's complied with, they will make new rules and excuses to complicate things. Such as, in the case study of Lucy. She may express she wants the child to see her father, but at the same time say it can't happen until a set a number of rules before that can happen, such as "'six weeks of phone calls" or a "mental examination". They are terrible communicators and are often desperate to confuse the process to hide their true intentions.

## No Contact

The narcissist will use emotional guilt and control to try to destroy your life and keep you confused. They want you to feel the they feel, broken. However, you will soon realise that resolution with these monsters is close to impossible. When you mess with a pig you will get dirty. Roll with dogs, you will get fleas. Stay well away. Resolution is futile with these losers. If you think you have resolved the situation with a narcissist, and when things seem to be going well, they will pull the rug from under you. The only resort is to go no contact. Have zero contact unless it is a formal setting.

## Grey Rock

If you need to speak or interact with the narcissist in a formal setting or perhaps a family gathering, you can use the Grey Rock method. This is where you nullify and dumb down your language and behaviour to simple one-word answers, emotionless tonality and simple rhetoric. Don't express any emotion, any opinions, any thoughts and don't show any distress (this will make them happy). Just be generic.

By being this way, they won't have anything to latch onto. Remember, they are trying to catch you out and they want to attack something. Don't give them that reason. Grey Rock is difficult to do because if you show discomfort or distress, the narcissist will enjoy it and will most likely call it out. It takes some practice. Try relaxing all of your facial expressions, keep your eyes relaxed, don't smile, don't frown and just be as monotone as you can.

## **<u>Hoovering</u>**

Watch out for hoovering. This is a way for the narcissist to get your attention when you have finally decided to go No Contact. As mentioned earlier in this book, they love attention, and they can't stand the fact that someone is refusing to give them time and attention. Them stalking you and provoking you is a way to smoke you out. They want you to react and they want to provoke you. Some actions they do are designed for you to react aggressively. Don't give them that luxury. They want your attention and they want to emotionally control you.

Your toxic ex will do everything possible to hoover you. They could openly brag and showcase their new partner, they can try to emotionally upset you by using your children, they can contact family members to ignite anger and resentment. They will even travel to your friends and family. It's all for provocation purposes.

It's very rare that a narcissist will hoover you in a good way, but it can happen. Perhaps they miss you and want to rope you back in so they can play their games with you again. Remember, you are a commodity to them, a financial gain and if they can get more from you then they will try.

## Summary

If you are about to break up with a narcissist or have already broke up, here are some things to expect and tools you can implement to help you understand what you're going through -

1. They will look to financially destroy you
2. They will use your children as a weapon to control you and emotionally damage you
3. They will provoke you. They want you to react violently or aggressively so they can use that against you in a formal setting. Don't fall for the trap. Don't react
4. They will stalk your social media. Don't share happy posts on public pages, your happiness will fuel revenge from them. Share happy posts in private pages with trusted friend bases
5. Make sure to go No Contact, any kind of deal with these monsters is futile
6. Be careful of hoovering, they will try to hoover you in negative and potentially positive ways. They want your attention, and they want to keep emotionally controlling you
7. If you need to interact with them, try to implement Grey Rock. Stay emotionless, monotone and don't give the narcissist an excuse or reason to attack you. They are desperate to attack you
8. Breaking up with a narcissist is a chaotic nightmare because of their tormented, lonely childhood with deep rooted abandonment issues. A breakup hits them differently and it is not a normal break up

## Exercise

What were the red flags which resulted in your relationship ending?

______________________________________________

______________________________________________

______________________________________________

______________________________________________

______________________________________________

______________________________________________

______________________________________________

______________________________________________

______________________________________________

How did the narcissist try to get revenge on you?

______________________________________________

______________________________________________

______________________________________________

______________________________________________

______________________________________________

______________________________________________

______________________________________________

______________________________________________

______________________________________________

## Notes

Write down any other thoughts here. What steps will you be taking to recover from your horrific breakup? Would you have done anything differently? What approach would you have taken if you could rerun the nightmare?

____________________________________________________

____________________________________________________

____________________________________________________

____________________________________________________

____________________________________________________

____________________________________________________

____________________________________________________

____________________________________________________

____________________________________________________

____________________________________________________

____________________________________________________

____________________________________________________

____________________________________________________

____________________________________________________

____________________________________________________

____________________________________________________

____________________________________________________

____________________________________________________

# CHAPTER 6
## TRIANGULATION AND HOW YOUR NETWORK IS BRAINWASHED

After the breakup, you will most likely encounter a major character assassination attempt and smear campaign. This is a way for the narcissist to maintain their appearance as the angel and make you appear to be the aggressor who has done everything wrong.

"How dare they not love me, how dare they not stay with me," is their default thought. They can't understand how you don't want to be with them and for this they want to punish you.

Hypothetically, if you have done everything correctly. Was never violent, no abuse, never cheated, never home drunk. Generally, the model partner, you'd question why they would have any problem with that. However, things are different with a narcissist and all they want is control. If post breakup they can't control you, they will look to destabilise you. Remember what we said, this is not a normal breakup and you are not dealing with a normal person.

Post relationship, expect an onslaught of passive aggressive attacks, mostly through other people. The narcissist will use your family as a way to attack you. They will visit them, mention subtle things to attack you and smear you. This is so natural to the narcissist, they may not fully appreciate or understand what they are doing is causing so much harm because harming others comes so natural to them.

* * *

Narcissists will go into your personal lifestyle and mention anything they can to subtly throw shots at you to others. They can use their friends to send you harassing messages and they will look to throw out petty jibes constantly. It's designed to try to character assassinate, the idea is to a) bully you b) smear and embarrass you, c) elevate themselves over you and d) to provoke you. They want you to lash out, they want you to react because it gives them more ammunition to use against you.

It's important for you to cope with the onslaught while not reacting. Feelings of revenge, bitterness and anger is very common and part of overthinking and being damaged by narcissistic abuse is those feelings of resentment. Just know, they are the ill ones, and they are the ones who are forever going to be miserable.

Try to see them as the victim and step away from your tormenting thoughts. You will not gain anything from over thinking the situation. Try to zone in on your comfort zone and keep your friends and family close to you. Talk about your problems and find therapy in discussing your problems, sharing your thoughts and delving into things that you enjoy doing. You will find there are other people experiencing similar things, and that can bring you comfort. In short, keep your mind off things, over thinking can get you into mental struggle. As the phrase goes, the devil has work for idle hands.

After a breakup with a narcissist, there is some positivity that will come from it. You will see who is there for you in times of need. Loyalty is a trait that can only be tested when huge amounts of stress is added, then you will see how far it will bend.

* * *

Post breakup, you will see what friends are naturally loyal to you. Usually from your group, one will empathise the most and will be there to provide a helping hand and offer advice on what you need to do.

In parallel, you will also see who doesn't care for you and who is against you. A neutral person will often see two sides of the story before providing constructive feedback. An enemy, or someone who is not on your side, will often only hear the narcissists opinion, and before giving you a chance to say your side of the story, will pass critical judgement.

"You did what?" they will ask. "I can't believe you could treat someone like this?" In response to something the narcissist has told them. This is an example of someone who is not for you, doesn't care for you and is against you.

Your network is most likely good-natured people who don't want to rock the boat and are often airing on the side of caution to keep the peace. However, the narcissist is not looking for peace and will use this as an opportunity to smear, attach, exploit and subtly play their psychological games.

Often, with triangulation, the third person doesn't want to be involved in the situation but are subtly coerced into being so. If children are involved, expect endless phone calls to speak to that person. It's guilt tripping and emotional manipulation.

In triangulation, the third person isn't aware of the game being played, they think they are just minding their own business. But the toxic narcissist, who has made a life of being the feeble, meek victim, has burrowed their way into their life also.

As discussed previously, don't react to it. The people who care for you will listen to you and will be there for you, the people who don't will make that very clear.

Toxic people come in all ways, whether you have broken up with them or have them in your circle of friends or family, they are suppressive. They don't want you to be happy, they don't want the best for you and these people are just trying to find ways to bring you down, attack you, lower your confidence and suppress you. It's all in the name of making themselves feel better, and usually stems from resentment and jealousy toward you.

As mentioned earlier, the narcissist is playing a game which you are not playing. They are smearing your name and trying to alleviate themselves. Try not to fall into the same traps. As frustrating as it is. They really do just want to lower you to their level. Sit back and let them play their game, the people who know you, the people who care for you and the people who want the best for you will reach out to you and speak with you before passing judgement. As for the others, take it as a gift, often people don't get the opportunity to see who is on their side and who really cares for them. If there is anything that will put that to the test, it's a narcissistic breakup.

## Summary

After breaking up with a narcissist, you will discover a lot about your family, friends and social circle and will have the opportunity to see who is for you and who is against you. Look out for these signs -

1. Triangulation. Narcissists will use innocent third parties to manipulate, smear you and character assassinate you
2. Narcissists will do everything to destroy your reputation and will dig up anything they can think of to throw out there
3. Narcissists are playing a game whereby they want to turn everyone against you. Try hard not to fall into the trap of lowering yourself to their level
4. Don't incriminate yourself. They want you to react so they can use it against you
5. Beware and be prepared for losing family and friends post narcissistic breakup. You will see who is supportive of you and who is willing to listen. Toxic people may emerge from other areas of your life (view this as a gift)

## Exercise

How did the narcissist try to manipulate your family, friends and network after the breakup?

_______________________________________________

_______________________________________________

_______________________________________________

_______________________________________________

_______________________________________________

_______________________________________________

_______________________________________________

_______________________________________________

_______________________________________________

Who from your family and friends were on your side and what did you learn from them?

_______________________________________________

_______________________________________________

_______________________________________________

_______________________________________________

_______________________________________________

_______________________________________________

_______________________________________________

_______________________________________________

## **Notes**

Write your thoughts here on triangulation and what you would do differently to avoid your family/network being brainwashed by the toxic narcissist.

# CHAPTER 7
# PICKING UP THE ASHES

After a breakup with a narcissist, you may feel like you are lost. Narcissists are experts at taking your happiness away and overtly relish in taking love away from you, in any way they can. They will do everything they can to sabotage your new relationships, your friendships, your family and if there are children involved, they will use them as a weapon.

Narcissists don't just take your happiness away, they take your soul. The reason for this is because they ingrain themselves so deeply into the fabrics of your life, like a trojan horse, they infiltrate your defense. The story of the trojan horse, just for context, and lightly paraphrased, is during a 10-year war named, 'The Trojan War', the Greeks entered the city of Troy in a deceptive manner. They created a wooden horse as a victory trophy for the Trojans, and the Greeks were seen sailing away. As the wooden horse was carted into the city, unbeknownst to the Trojan's, there were Greek soldiers hidden inside who then attacked once inside the city. The same principle applies with covert narcissists, such is their passive aggressive and conniving nature, they will infiltrate your defenses, get into your personal life space and then look to attack it from the inside.

Your breakup has been a whirlwind; it has crashed and burned with your family and friends observing the carnage. You have been traumatized and recovering from it will not be easy. It's like you have been injected with a poison and that poison needs to leave your body. Imagine narcissists to be like the character *Venom* from the *Spiderman* movies. When Venom touches something, it turns into them. We could go even more philosophical and quote Nietzsche when he said, "When you gaze into the abyss, the abyss also gazes into you," which translates to, corruption makes people corrupt. If you are not aware of what is across from you, it will poison you.

After the breakup, you will be poisoned and all you can think about is how to resolve the situation, how to move on, but the narcissist isn't letting you move on. They keep coming back with more hate, they may use their children against you, they may smear your name and try attacking you from afar. They are not willing to talk to you to resolve the situation. What can be resolved with a simple message of, "Ok, enough is enough, let's sort this out," is replaced with silence, confusing messages and emotional manipulation.

They are constantly moving the goal posts. One minute it's one condition, next minute it's another, one minute they want something, next minute not. They are playing a game. Why? Because they are probably hurt too. A narcissist doesn't take rejection well. They believe they are royalty, so the thought of anyone rejecting them is met with pure hatred. It could result in you getting physically attacked as well as psychologically.

* * *

You are in this situation, trying to heal, trying to move on, trying to make sense of what has happened, but it's difficult because you are dealing with an irrational being. Someone who is incapable of having a responsible, dignified conversation with you. Remember what we said earlier, they are poor communicators, they won't know exactly how to portray their feelings, and, terrified of their true self emerging, they lock themselves away and in the end, say very little.

You've been poisoned in this whirlwind and you need to detoxify. We talk about No Contact a lot, but what does it really mean? It means your soul needs to heal. You have been taking this psychological drug and in an odd way, it's addictive! As torturous as it is, your body is stimulated by the narcissists heightened level of argumentative style. This is why people from tortured pasts always find trouble. Deep down, they are somewhat addicted to it.

You need to detoxify and cleanse your soul. Stay well away from the narcissist, even if you have kids, if you've tried for years to have a relationship and if you've done everything short of jumping through a ring of fire and climbing a building in a batman costume, don't pander to the narcissist's games. They are selfish, lack empathy, poor communicators and if they really wanted to resolve a situation with you, they would reach out. The pride of someone who thinks they are perfect is difficult to repair once you reject them. Just for you not being interested in them, is a death sentence in their eyes. They cannot accept it. Normal people are hurt for a few weeks and then they move on, but for toxic people with abandonment issues, it will likely end in them having a life-long vendetta against you. Remember, protect yourself and try to be safe, your life could be at risk.

Detoxify, cleanse your soul and the only way you can do that is to not have any interaction with them. Over time, you will feel those feelings of rage and vengefulness slowly dissipate. Those feelings of fear will slowly evaporate. Your soul will heal, day by day, you will find your mojo and your smile will come back. It's not easy, but keep telling yourself about this poison being inside you and the only way it can go is if you have no more contact with it.

One of the keys to success is to not get involved with a narcissist in the first place, and this is very difficult to pre-empt. For the reasons we've discussed, they are extremely deceptive people. It takes planning and skill to avoid being trapped in a narcissistic relationship, but there are a few things you can do.

Make sure to share very little with your partner, avoid joint mortgages, avoid joint bank accounts, try to keep your lives as separate as possible. Make sure they have their own friends, don't share friends and keep things independent. This way, if the relationship breaks up (which most do), it will make things slightly more manageable when the attacks start happening.

You may be feeling lost and broken after a narcissistic relationship, but it is possible to regain focus and rebuild the new you. Take it as a challenge to build the 2.0 version of yourself. You have to emotionally, spiritually and physically reconnect with who you are and start to rebuild.

Before we dig into some of the steps you can take to achieve that, you have to go No Contact from the narcissist. You can't have that nightmare lingering in the background. It will torture and torment you. If you have kids, you will have to make a difficult decision. The balance is, try to have a relationship with your kids, but you will have to do this without any interaction with the narcissist. You simply cannot move on with their voice, their messages and their toxic passive aggressive tactics constantly and relentlessly trying to catch you out and disrupt your life. Remember, they don't want you to be happy and your happiness and success will fuel their jealousy to attack you more. They are stalking your every move so don't expect any compromise from them. They are an enemy for life and therefore, for you to truly move on, you need to cut that cord. The ship can only sail when the rope to the shore is cut. You can only climb a mountain once the giant boulder on your back is cut loose.

In my book, *10 Steps To Heal From Narcissistic Abuse,* which is included for free in this book (page number is in the Table Of Contents), I go through 10 steps that can be used to build the 2.0 version of yourself. It will take commitment and it will require accountability, but they can be used as a guideline to track against. Measuring your progress is important and hopefully the questions in this book will help you write down your thoughts and help you monitor the steps you are taking to regain control.

Let's go through the 10 Steps and get a brief view and summary of what they are.

## <u>Regain Control of Your Life</u>

Regain control of your life. Spending a sustained amount of time with a narcissist automatically results in abuse because they control almost every area of your life. Even if they mean to do it or not (its often natural to them as they are innately toxic). This will have you feeling powerless and somewhat out of control of your own life. Now is the time to change that, you hold the keys now. You can decide who you want to be, you can decide what you want your life to be and You can decide your future. Don't let the narcissist control you anymore. They can do this emotionally, by trying to hoover you, you may feel that warm feeling of happiness when they try to worm their way back into your life. Don't fall for it. If you have co-dependent tendencies, you need to recognise that and seek help for it. Remember what we discussed earlier in the book, co-dependency can go in multiple directions, seek the healthy path.

## Let go of the Past

Moving on is the only way to have a bright future. Letting go of the past, as frustrating and gut wrenching as it is, is important and you have to let go. The world is imperfect and there are imperfect people in it, including yourself. People will make mistakes to you and you will make mistakes to others. You can't control other people, but you can control how you respond and react. Let go of the extra weight that is slowing you down. When you truly do that, you can start sprinting to a bright future.

## Trust Your Gut Instinct

Our fight or flight instincts have been forged through years and years of evolution and guess what? They work! Your gut is one of the most powerful intuition tools, it's just often we don't listen to it. Empaths will be more open to their intuition and often have a greater sense for someone's energy (whether positive or negative). It can be classified as a sixth sense and should be harnessed. As great a gift as it is, it can also be a burden. Absorbing the energy of someone who has negative feelings toward you is exhausting and it can lead to overthinking. Harness this power, manage the feelings, treat it like a superpower and always trust it. Your intuition (gut instinct) is an immensely powerful tool.

## Find Your Vice / Find Your Purpose in Life

Often finding our purpose in life gives us something to wake up to. We have a mission in life that keeps us occupied. After a narcissistic break up, you really are just constantly looking over your shoulder for when the next attack is going to come. The feelings of resentment, hate and fear can overwhelm you and this is exhausting to the point you may not want to do much in your life. In short, you will become depressed. I know of people who lock themselves in their home as a security blanket and their passion, goals and previous hobbies were all parked while they tried to weather the storm of abuse and emotions brought on by the evil narcissist.

## Choose Your Friends Wisely / Go No Contact

After breaking up with a narcissist, you will most likely get an exceptionally good idea on who is with you and who is against you. This will include family members. A toxic relationship will weed out the fakes in your life who secretly want to see you fail. Those who trust you will ask for your opinion and will offer guidance. They want to help. Those who couldn't give two cahoots about you, will believe the narcissist, side with the narcissist and/or remain "neutral". Expect some to say things like, "I'm in the middle, I don't want to take sides," or, "I don't want to get involved." Whilst all the while, they are involved by default because the toxic narcissist is involving them, and they are facilitating and compliant in the narcissist's games. Choose your friends wisely, keep your circle small and ensure you are surrounded by loyal confidants who have your back.

## Research the Topic of Narcissism

Knowledge is power. As the saying goes, but it's true. The more you know, the more you can analyse situations and the closer you will be to a favourable outcome. Knowledge doesn't solve everything, it has to be used as a supplementary tool in your armory, but it is nonetheless powerful. Research narcissism, read books like this, watch YouTube videos, buy other books, speak to your friends about it, write articles. Absorb as much information as you can. By knowing the red flags, you will be in prime position to pre-empt issues, avoid drama, avoid chaos and avoid a narcissistic relationship. Furthermore, if you find yourself in a narcissistic relationship, you will identify the red flags early and will be able to react. Narcissism and narcissistic abuse are still relatively niche topics. Learn as much as you can and get a head start on what you could be dealing with.

## Set Boundaries

What happens when there are no rules? Anarchy emerges. This is the same concept you can use when thinking about boundaries. Boundaries are your own personal rulebook. Lines people can't cross. Often, we let people passive aggressively exploit us in the spirit of *not wanting conflict* but what that is doing is just causing more confusion and resentment. If you have failed to shut down a blatant act to offend you then that needs to change. It's not being sensitive if you are offended, narcissists will use that card of, "Oh, don't you know how to take a joke?" or, "calm down, I'm just kidding." However, there has to be boundaries so the other person knows they can't hurt your feelings. They don't know what goes on in your mind, and different things land differently with others.

We are not all the same. So, therefore, don't feel guilty. If anyone crosses a line with you, point your finger at them and tell them, unequivocally, "I will not tolerate you speaking to me like that, okay? You cannot speak to me like that. Do you understand?" Make sure not to threaten them or give them a reason to gaslight you and accuse *you* of being offensive. They will always try to divert. Just a simple, concise message (you can leave out the finger pointing to not be as confrontational) will usually do the trick. Let them know you can't be messed with. Remember, don't always try to be liked, be respected.

## **Accept the Situation / Be Honest with Yourself**

Things will happen in your life which are so atrocious you may question why they happened to you. Your life could have been so much more relaxed and calmer if you didn't meet that particular person or if you had made a different decision at some point in your life. One of the comforting things when analysing your own horrific situation is, there are millions of others in the same boat! Life can be unfair, and life can be difficult. Things don't always work out the way you want them to. Look at some of the most successful people in history, Steve Jobs, Elon Musk, Tom Cruise, Jeff Bezos. They have all gone through divorces or breakups and are possibly paying through-the-roof in child support to a vengeful ex-partner. Life isn't perfect. Some of our favourite celebrities who we look up to have gone through horrific adversity which are irreversible and, in many cases, forever out there in the public eye. A lot of people have problems and though this doesn't fix your situation, it's a good perspective to know you are not alone.

During these situations, it's important to be honest with yourself. Did you do everything the right way? What mistakes did you make? How would you change your behaviour? No one is perfect. We all make mistakes and at times we can go low too. Nobody is Jesus, except for Jesus himself!

The narcissistic viewpoint would be to suggest they did everything perfect and 100% of the blame is on the other person. That's how narcissist's think and possibly the narcissist in your life thinks that way. Remember what we said earlier, they take no blame and will never say sorry. Accountability is a myth to these people.

It's important to accept you may be imperfect but also accept you want to improve and get better. In parallel, you are not alone, people have it worse. If you were to ask someone else to exchange problems, they may do so in a heartbeat.

## <u>Change Your Paradigm</u>

Perspective is very important, similar to our previous step, we can take comfort in knowing you are not alone and there are millions of others going through the same things. In parallel, it's important to understand it is the aggression of the other person who is causing the chaos and it is *them* who is mentally ill. For sure, during a breakup and any involvement with a narcissist, your life will be uncomfortable if you are forced to be around them. Focus on your paradigm and focus on the rule. Stay No Contact, don't rise to their provocations, use their negative energy to motivate you to do greater things and understand it is them who are miserable, toxic and bitter. They are the ones who require mental help. Perspective is everything, and your life is not that bad. Just make sure your mind doesn't become your biggest enemy. Look for ways to relieve pressure, have fun, enjoy your life, be happy and know you have done everything you can. Sometimes, you can't fix everything. Remember, if you wrestle with a pig, you will get dirty. It will come a point when you will have to stop wrestling.

## **<u>Let go and Have Fun!</u>**

Sometimes you just need to let go. Those negative thoughts will keep you awake at night and it will serve you no purpose. It's understandable that your mind is trying to process a complex situation, but it will come a point when you can't do this alone. It will take the other person (the narcissist) to meet you in the middle, and if that is not happening, you need to let go. You can't be the only one banging on the door until your fist starts to bleed. Everything has a limit.

Once you know you've done everything you can, you need to find that new direction in your life and go for it! Be a bit selfish, the toxic person in your life has imprisoned you for too long. Toxic negative people have accused you of being certain things in the past, but we've already established they are not on your side. They are not for you, they are against you. Once you know who the people on your side are, you can weed out the negativity and focus on being the best version of you. Be happy, be proud of who you are, work hard, be healthy, help others, have dreams, have ambitions and try to include everyone in the success you are trying to build. If a toxic partner is blocking certain things, manipulating you and trying to have you act like a circus animal then, well, the answer is simple. Don't let them control you. They don't know how to compromise or meet in the middle, they just want everything their own way, like the king or queen of their *Kingdom*, they are 100% uncompromising.

The sooner you realise the red flags of these people, the sooner you can cut the cord and live your life. The right people will find their way into your life when the time is right. You can have and you deserve a bright future.

## Exercise

What three steps are you going to begin with and take action on?

_______________________________________________

_______________________________________________

_______________________________________________

_______________________________________________

_______________________________________________

_______________________________________________

_______________________________________________

_______________________________________________

How will you measure this? I need you to be accountable for these steps, what will you do to ensure you stick to them?

_______________________________________________

_______________________________________________

_______________________________________________

_______________________________________________

_______________________________________________

_______________________________________________

_______________________________________________

_______________________________________________

Who is the person you want to be in 5 years?

## Notes

Write your thoughts on any other steps you can take to build a 2.0 version of yourself. What is your wish list moving forward and how will you achieve them?

# CHAPTER 8
## A DIVINE FUTURE

They say time is the ultimate healer. With time, the memories of the past can dissolve and even your fondest memories can often feel like dreams. A study on memory once revealed your recollection of a memory is dependent on the tweaks and subtle changes you made when discussing the event to others. If you've added a slight embellishment to your story to make it sound more interesting, which is common for people to do, then over time, you may have convinced yourself that the event happened to how you were describing it.

The time premise can be translated to negative memories. With time, it dissipates into a dream-like memory and what you're left with are the feelings and thoughts you were experiencing when telling yourself the encounter. This can be good or bad, of course, but there's an argument to be made that over time, your nightmare thoughts become vague, colourless and don't quite carry the same punch they once did.

Using the 10 Step program, you can build a new you and find happiness, calm and prosperity in your present and forthcoming life. To do this you have to be relentless. You can't be lukewarm with your approach, you have to set strong boundaries and don't let anyone cross them under any circumstances. That militant approach to your mental health and well being will put you in good stead and you will gain respect for it. From others, and your-self.

Narcissists don't know how to respect others, they will show constant contempt to you and others around them. Heck, they don't even respect themselves, why should you expect any from them? You can spend months rebuilding your thought process, energy and self-esteem, but one encounter with a toxic narcissist will plunge you back into the abyss again. They only know how to criticise. You may not see them for months and you may be committed to Grey Rocking the conversation, but they will still find a way to criticise you.

One example to articulate this is an exchange I heard from one of our students with a toxic family member. After six months of No Contact, they were forced to engage a few words. Our student explained the narcissist didn't engage with a welcome, rather, it was the target who politely asked how things were and was met with a defensive reaction.

"Hey, how's it going. I heard you weren't well. Are you ok?"

"Wait, what? What are you on about?" the narcissist replies with a scrunched-up face.

"No, I just heard you weren't well."

"Oh."

Narcissists are always on the defensive and want to control the conversation. It's only a matter of time when criticism will be levelled toward you, and in this situation, it arrived. After months of no contact or refusal for polite rapport, they managed to criti-cise, *wait for it*, the targets dog's balls!

Apparently, his dogs ball sack was "too red and requires ur-gent medical attention."

I'm told the dog is a scrambly Yorkshire terrier and at times, for better or worse, rubs his never regions onto the carpet! Not much else to say, really. It just highlights that when a narcissist doesn't like you, regardless of how much time has passed, they will find something to criticise!

The lesson here is, minimise the contact with toxic people so you can work on your divine future (and present life). Stick to the 10 steps and be ruthless with your boundaries. Over time, you will see the attempted attacks become even more frivolous, groundless and desperate.

## **<u>Triggers</u>**

One of the difficult things when moving on is getting passed your vengeful, bitter thoughts. It's easy to feel that way and I know we've discussed the importance of acceptance, but it's also important to understand what is triggering the feelings you're getting.

Often, it can be something very left field which is triggering your emotions. Something you may not necessarily be consciously thinking of all the time. It can be something as simple as how you look. If you've gained weight or overeaten, then that might be a trigger that ignites depressed and self-esteem issues. If you struggle with relationships and have been let down by a potential new date, that can be a trigger. If, and I'm sure you can relate to this, a particular person's name is mentioned, then that could trigger passionate emotions.

Be honest with yourself and try to identify the emotional triggers. By zoning in on this, it can help you manage your mind-state better until one day, those thoughts and memories will dissolve into a vague after thought.

## __Your Past, Present and Future__

There is an exercise you can do to help you get an objective view of yourself and really map out the trigger points in your life that have affected you. I tried this task myself and it really helped bring some of my inner thoughts and insecurities to the surface.

Firstly, I want you to get a pen and paper, or your laptop/computer and write down the story of your childhood. Write what you did, what it was like, what stuff you did. And most importantly, write what made you happy, any specific events that brought a smile to your face and also anything that made you sad or situations that made you very upset. Write down why it made you upset and how it made you feel. Write from the years you can remember.

This exercise will help you get to the root cause of specific events that trigger you, to this day, and it will help you understand why you're feeling certain things and why you're longing for certain types of attention.

Once you've done that, I then want you to write the story of your present. What is life currently like? What makes you happy? What makes you upset? Repeat the process, write down why you feel happy and why you feel sad, write your inner thoughts and feelings to certain things, and write down what your reactions are. Are you doing what you want to do in your present life? If yes, great, if not, what is it you'd rather be doing?

This transitions nicely to the third part of this exercise. Your future. What is your ideal future? What would you love to be doing in five, ten or fifteen years time? Make sure to keep it realistic, nothing too outlandish like, "I want to fly to Mars," or, "I want to win the lottery."

Write some goals of yours that you want to achieve, and these can be ambitious. You want to write a screenplay and try and get it viewed by millions? You want to run a private equity firm and have your own office? You want to donate money and help starving children around the world? What can you see yourself doing, what would make you happy? This could be something as simple as having a loving family, a nice home, two cars on the driveway and lots of kids running around. It doesn't have to be materialistic.

Once you've written your past, present and future. I'm confident this will give you a new perspective on what's been missing in your life and what it is you're longing for.

*  *  *

To finish this portion of the book, I want to discuss with you the idea of Existentialism. This was a theory born from Europe in the 19th century and shaped by multiple philosophers, one of which was Frederick Nietzsche. The idea stems from the theory we merely exist in this world as a physical being, in control of who we are, independent and not bound by external rules. We, as an independent being, are free to develop ourselves with free will. Often what controls us is the idea of *how we should behave* in certain situations and this universal morality that hovers over us. The truth is a lot of those ideas are man made. Of course, we must adhere to the laws and we must be a good person, this is important.

This ideal of a life, to go to college, get a job, get married, have kids etc. is just a false ideal. No one should feel inferior if they don't have these things. It doesn't define who you are or your level of success. Your level of success is defined by you. What do you want to achieve? To some, achievement is helping other people or reaching a particular goal. To others, achievement is something slightly different.

Existentialists believe in the idea of 'Absurd'. Which translates to the idea that the world and the universe doesn't appear to have any meaning. In short, we're not that important! We are on a floating planet in a seemingly infinite universe and the problems we have created for ourselves aren't really that important in the grand scheme of things. Again, it goes back to this idea of trying to fit your life into the cookie-cutter ideals that we've been taught, but in truth, there is no right or wrong. We merely exist and your existence is the only thing you should focus on.

Now, of course, it's important to build good relationships, have a loving family, friends and be a good person. Existentialism doesn't have to be a theory in selfishness, but it's also important to understand that, for the most part, life will be what it will be. Don't kill yourself trying to fit your life into a cookie-cutter mold. If things are to be, they will be. As a great song writer once said, "the best songs write themselves," perhaps even the best movies write themselves. They don't require too much thought, they simply fall into place. The idea of the absurd is we get upset over things, for example, money, gossip and whatever else, but that in itself is absurd as we are already living in a somewhat meaningless world.

The idea of Existentialism is to remove the noise and chaos from your life and focus your energies on positive things. Goals, plans, being a good person, great relationships and focus on your journey in life while in parallel detoxifying from the poison the past has injected in you.

I can't confirm if things happen for a reason, but over time, if you are committed, your life will land in the right place and you will be doing what you are destined to do. The right people will find their way into your life and what will be, will be.

Life goes on, and to close, in the words of Hunter S. Thompson, "We are a sum total of all of our reactions to the experiences we have had."

## **Exercise**

What memories from your past trigger you and what will you do to try to combat that?

_______________________________________________

_______________________________________________

_______________________________________________

_______________________________________________

_______________________________________________

_______________________________________________

_______________________________________________

_______________________________________________

_______________________________________________

What is your ideal future? Where do you want to be in 10 years?

_______________________________________________

_______________________________________________

_______________________________________________

_______________________________________________

_______________________________________________

_______________________________________________

_______________________________________________

_______________________________________________

_______________________________________________

What are your thoughts on Existentialism? Is it a philosophy you will look into further?

## Notes

In this section, write any closing thoughts on this book. What are your views on narcissistic relationships? What will you do different to try to avoid them? How will you manage the situation if you found yourself to be involved with one and how will you handle situations when in the same company as a narcissistic couple?

# 10 STEPS TO HEAL FROM NARCISSISTIC ABUSE

# INTRODUCTION

What is narcissism? The word has traditionally been associated with a harmless love for one's self, very rarely being used to describe a destructive abuse mechanism. When mainstream society thinks of narcissism, I get the feeling it's not looked at with disdain, but rather as an off-the-cuff petty character trait. How wrong could it be?

The world we live in has become narcissistic. Driven by materialism and superficial goals, no longer does humanity wish to work in communities, but rather to bring people down - society judges people by what car they drive, what job they have, how much money they make, what clothes they wear, what their face looks like, what their voice sounds like, what shoes they wear, what phone they have, what area of town they live in. The list goes on and on. A narcissist will judge all of these things. They are too shallow to consider anything else. They don't want to work as a team; they are driven by jealousy and seek vengeance on anyone happy with their lives.

If you're reading this now, you know better than to disregard the danger, weight, and severity of a narcissistic person. You may have encountered such people, encounters which have brought you to this very book. If you've been unlucky, you may have suffered the wrath of the narcissist. If you are this person, the contents of this book will be for you. Narcissists, and toxic people in general, do not have a petty off-the-cuff character trait. They are controlling, torturous, soul-destroying black holes of society.

The World we live in has gone down that path and, as a result, all of humanity, certainly in the developed World, is on the Narcissistic Spectrum. Having a healthy self-esteem and being proud of who you are and your achievements is a good thing. Having a healthy competition with your friends and colleagues to out-do each other and maintain a healthy respect while doing it is good. It's all part of the competition of life and it's the way it should be.

The extreme side of narcissism is toward the end of the spectrum, where it becomes toxic. This is known as Narcissistic Personality Disorder. These people don't wish you well; they don't acknowledge anything you do that could be perceived as successful nor will they encourage you. They are terrified at the prospect of someone being happier and more successful than them. They are jealous people, to the bone. What they fail to recognize is that happiness and success are subjective and are in the eye of the beholder. But Narcissists believe the world revolves around them in a egotistical and superficial way. All they do is look for ways to ridicule you.

This one person who I once knew was one of the worst cases of covert narcissism I have ever seen. We had mutual friends, and at various gatherings I was forced to be in the same room as him. He was never invited to my parties, but he weaselled his way in. I barely spoke to the guy, but he'd make fun of my voice to colleagues (in the name of jest). He'd make fun of my home and criticise elements of it. He criticised a mobile app I once made. He ridiculed my car. I once found he even ridiculed my appearance. All of this was in the name of 'jest'. That's what these people do; they don't confront you face to face; they pretend to be a 'friend'. They hide and lurk in the shadows like the scum they are, and they will look to attack you from afar. Everything they do is covert bullying, but its designed to a) be disguised, b) ruin your reputation, and c) encourage you to attack.

They want you to strike out. They want you to react. This gives them power. This gives them something to talk about. The truth is, these narcissists are very jealous, insecure people. They often come from broken homes, broken relationships, and are cripplingly dull individuals in constant search for 'supply' – i.e. praise and admiration. Without it, they can't cope. This particular person was like the Talented Mr. Ripley. He literally tried to copy everything I did, but in secret did everything to bring me down.

The tools I discuss in this book are tools I've used to get my *own* life back. I was at rock bottom. I couldn't sleep. I couldn't think. I felt angry, vengeful, and ultimately, just helpless. I felt like every word was weighed and every move was measured. There was nowhere to go. I couldn't think of or say anything without it being scrutinized. The poison from the narcissist affected me, specifically from an ex girlfriend, and it poisoned my soul. I lost myself. I wasn't the same person any longer; my spirit had been darkened. To this day, I still feel the remnants of that time. You never forget the emotional damage; it never quite leaves you. It's there, but in this book, you will see the methods and changes I made to get my life back - to get my spirit back, to get my direction back, and to ultimately fight back against the Narcissist and Flying Monkeys (I'll explain what that is later).

It took me years to feel happy again; there was a lot of research and discovery involved. But you won't have to do what I did. I'm going to share with you my tricks and my techniques so you won't have to wait years. The 10 Step program I propose in this book will help you see changes in your life immediately – it will require commitment and a new outlook in some areas, but stick with it. Rome wasn't built in a day.

# GLOSSARY OF TERMS

To help us further familiarise ourselves with the key traits of a Narcissist (and toxic people), here are a few character traits and behaviours in which they engage:

**Gaslighting**

Gaslighting is an expression to describe when an individual meticulously manipulates the target into thinking they are losing their mind. Narcissists and toxic people in general use gaslighting as one way to deflect attention away from themselves, causing the victim to go stir crazy, questioning whether they themselves are the crazy ones. Narcissists and toxic people will lie, manipulate, control and fabricate situations to instil self-doubt. They will manipulate other people to have the same views as them, and these views will be expressed to the target.

The term Gaslighting originally came from a movie called Gaslight, which was first created in 1940 and then remade for the big screen in 1944. It won several awards and raised awareness of psychological manipulation.

Let's explore a few hypothetical situations. Imagine if someone was to accuse someone of having Autism and told this to the target continuously, whilst also convincing other people of this person's apparent 'autism' and had them accuse the target of it, too. Then with repeat accusation, positioned in a 'caring and thoughtful' way, this might just start to drive the target crazy, forcing them to think and question themselves as to whether they have autism. Not the best example, but it is a form of social conditioning that can be manufactured by a narcissist or toxic person. *Yes, they are sick enough to do such a thing!*

Another example, from my fiction novel *The Devil In I*, is a situation where the main character, Damon West, is infatuated with another woman whilst in a relationship with his girlfriend, Stephanie. Stephanie suspects Damon of being distant with her, and she is right to think that. But Damon is so charming that he is able to deceive her and convince her she is just being paranoid. This started a downward spiral for Stephanie, as she knew something was wrong but couldn't pinpoint Damon to a crime. Unfortunately for Stephanie, things didn't end up so good! She literally went insane.

That's what Gaslighting can do to someone. It can make them question their sanity, make them paranoid, make them feel crazy, and essentially, things will spiral out of control for the unfortunate target.

## Ghosting

Ghosting is an emotional control tactic the Narcissist uses to get inside your head and emotionally hurt you. They will focus a lot of attention on you, taking up your time and attention, only to suddenly pull the carpet away and disappear.

Everyone has self-esteem in varying degrees, and Ghosting is an action which will damage that self-esteem. It will make you question, 'Why did they just disappear?'; "Was it something I did?"; "Was it the recent picture I sent them?"; "Was it something I said?"

Generally, toxic people will do Ghosting, but I've noticed in modern society, it is a relatively common human trait. It stems from the notion that somebody would invest a lot of time in someone, literally hours of communication, lots of interest and making the person believe there is a chance of a meaningful relationship. However, at some point, at the drop of a hat, that person will cease all contact with you. No explanation, no follow up message, no reason provided. Just nothing. That's an action called Ghosting and is extremely damaging to the unfortunate target.

It will make the target question whether they have done anything wrong. It will potentially lower their self esteem and confidence. It could lead to cynicism when meeting new people and could lead to those people building walls around themselves to protect themselves from the hurt of being emotionally invested in someone, only to be ditched at the drop of a hat.

Ghosting is not a nice thing to do, and anyone with courtesy, respect, and empathy for their human companions will at least send a message to make it clear how they are feeling. However, narcissists and toxic people don't have courtesy, respect, empathy, or integrity. They are cold, shallow individuals who don't care about other people, and they feel no remorse for hurting other people's feelings.

**Hoovering**

Hoovering is the term used for when the Narcissist or toxic person who was once in your life tries to come back! The best way to cure yourself from a toxic person is to go No Contact. Visually, on the Internet, telephone, any way possible, just cut all contact. But this isn't always the easiest thing to do. Narcissists are extremely charming and manipulative people. Their whole life is based on getting what they want, and they've set up their personality to facilitate that – and largely they are very good at getting their own way at the expense of others. In short, if you go No Contact with a Narcissist then take away that interaction the narcissist was so addicted to, they will come back for more. The target of a narcissist is a form of supply. Narcs fuel off this supply – the attention, the passion, the admiration. It's fuel for them. When it goes away, like a drug, the narc will crave more and will come back for more.

Whether it's one month or one year, the narcissist will always come back. They never go away. Sadly. They will go through extreme lengths to speak and interact with you. Anything to grab your attention. To lure you out of No Contact.

Expect every dirty tactic in the book. Fake profile names, fake numbers, fake emails, suicide attempts, threats to your life, threats to your family, threats to your home, smear campaigns, love bombing, legal action, hacking, phone tapping, bullying, stalking, social media messages….it goes on and on and on. Think of any way a person can get contacted or lured out of No Contact and the Narcissist will explore it. If a carrier pigeon with a camera attached to their head was possible, they'd do that, too.

## Love Bombing

Love Bombing is something a Narcissist does at several phases of a relationship. They do it at the beginning of a relationship, which is also known as an Over-Evaluation phase for them. This is where they shower their target with praise and admiration.

"Oh, you look so great today!", "I love your hair", "I like guys with wide shoulders", "I admire your hard work", "You're so funny."

Literally, they send endless compliments. This is a manipulation tool. The target will start to react positively to the praise. Just like they do with experiments on lab rats, where scientists put a piece of food into an area of the cage every 15 minutes – the lab rat would eventually go to that area of the cage and wait for the food every 15 minutes. It has been conditioned to go to that area because it knows there will be food there. That may not be the best example, but the target of this 'praise' from the narcissist will go to the narc for more. It becomes addictive and welcomed. The narcissist does this to keep people close, but also to have people dependent on them. This creates a problem for the Narcissist because ultimately, they lack empathy and don't care for anyone. Having a dependent is a real issue for them – a burden, so to speak. This leads to another phase of the relationship, which is De-valuing the person they've just been love bombing for the past five months. Literally, as mentioned in previous sections of this glossary, ditching them like last week's pizza.

Love Bombing is a powerful manipulation tool, and it also is used at other stages of the relationship. Narcissists will throw love bombs during a relationship following an argument. Additionally, they will want to move very quickly in a relationship. Within days they will want to get married, move in, have kids, plan the wedding, name the kids. Yes, it's that ridiculous. They want to tie the target in to a long-term commitment. But the vicious paradigm is that they themselves don't want the long-term commitment; it's doomed to fail. Narcissists don't want dependents, but they create them! This is what makes them so evil. They get people to fall in love with them so convincingly, yet all the while, their intention is to ditch the target.

## Flying Monkeys

You may have heard this term in the past and wondered, 'what is a flying monkey??' I know what you're thinking; it's slightly kooky sounding, but it really is a term used in psychology. I think it comes from the *Wizard of Oz* and the 'monkeys' that did the Witch's dirty deeds. In it's rawest form, that is what a Flying Monkey, in the psychology perspective, relates to.

A narcissist is an extremely manipulative person. They need people around them to devour them and hang on in every way. Servants, essentially, but specifically a source of narcissistic supply for the narcissist. This is another term, which relates to the narcissist's desire to constantly have praise heaped on them, in whatever way they can get it. They are constantly seeking validation from others because they hate themselves. The 'narcissistic supply' is, to a narcissist, as blood would be to a vampire. A very fitting comparison, I believe.

The flying monkey is part of the narcissist's immediate group. They are the minions, the henchmen of the narcissist. Now, they may have their own psychological issues with the narcissist. They may have a deep love for the narcissist and feel they have a chance with them for something 'meaningful'. They may feel a sense of status validation when around the narcissist – after all, narcissists are usually popular and well-liked people. Their whole facade and fake persona is a hit in social groups. A 'flying monkey' could be someone low in confidence, not as popular as the narcissist, and may find some strength being under the wing of the evil narcissist.

Either way, whatever the situation, the flying monkeys love and adore the narcissist. Anything the narcissist says, they will support it. Anything bad the narcissist does, for example, let's just hypothetically say cheating with multiple married men over several years or bullying someone to the point of becoming suicidal, the flying monkey will support and actually heap praise on the narcissist. One step further, they will ridicule the target in whatever has happened. Flying monkeys are loyal, I'll give them that much!

When you have an issue with a narcissistic person, you need to identify who their 'flying monkeys' are. Who are their closest allies? Who are they closest to? This is deceptive, because the minions will still try to be your friend – they are equally manipulative and deceptive. In fact, they are just as dangerous as the narcissist. They're part of the club! They know the game.

It's very normal for you to be friends with a flying monkey without realising that, behind the facade, they are talking bad about you and feeding the narcissist information about your every move. Narcissists are stalkers; they are like Mi5 agents. They find out everything, and one of the ways they do that is by using people, specifically their 'flying monkeys', to gather the information. This is a perfect situation for the narcissist because they are not in the line of fire. Things can't directly be linked back to them. Which is perfect for the narcissists' reputation. Remember, narcissists need a good reputation; they will do anything to savour it.

In summary, a flying monkey is a close ally of the narcissist and is just as dangerous and deceptive. If you're going no contact from a narcissist, go no contact with anyone associated with them, also.


## Smear Campaign

Narcissists come in many forms. They can be your 'friends', family, co-workers, lovers, doctors, teachers. They are everywhere in society. One may argue that society has helped influence the creation of self obsessed narcissists, but that's a different topic. Two key traits of a narcissist are jealousy and control. Believe it or not, those two things are a deadly combination. When a narcissist is envious of you, they want to smear your name (among other things). They want others to know how 'horrible' you are, how 'deluded' you are, how 'stupid' you are, how 'despicable and childish' you are.

What's interesting is, everything they accuse you of, is most probably a trait of their own. What makes a smear campaign more dangerous, is it's done sneakily and in disguise. You won't even know it's happened.

The narcissist will discuss how 'laughable and ridiculous' you are as a human with their 'flying monkey's (more on that later) – they will all have a laugh and a joke about how 'pathetic' you are. However, oddly, to your face, the narcissist and flying monkeys will be relatively civil and nice to you. They are jackals, two faced spineless losers who wouldn't be able to confront you if their life depended on it.

Obviously, there are a lot of variables, and there will be times when a narcissist will snap at you – but this if often behind closed doors.

The narcissist attempts to control the people around them, and they do this by ridiculing others. They are the ring leader of that action. Oddly enough, 'gossip' is a powerful manipulation tool. Everyone loves juicy gossip. Tabloid media and 'fake news' is dependent on it. People love gossip. The good news doesn't really sell. So, the narcissist uses this shallow tabloid media style to keep people close. If they are the source of 'fake news and juicy gossip', then people will gravitate to it. It's a conversation starter, "Did you hear about what he said yesterday?" "Did you hear about who slept with who last week?" etc, etc.

Narcissists are control freaks; they are also incredibly jealous and insecure. Sadly, if you are a secure, confident person with integrity and self respect – if you have more material things than a narcissist, they will seek to destroy your reputation at any cost.

The one way to mitigate this is to simply stay away from them visually and digitally. Don't expose yourself to them in any way. Go No Contact and close the door to your life to them. I will go into more detail on how to do this later in this book.

## Narcissistic Rage

Narcissists are all about maintaining appearances. Their marriage, their home, their physical appearance, their material things, their career – everything they have is a show. It's a facade to show the people around them how 'amazing and perfect' they are. So in public, you're relatively safe with them. Of course, they will come out with passive aggressive comments in public to embarrass you. If they are overt, they may even resort to full blown bullying. But more often than not, the Narcissist is not going to incriminate themselves in public, so mostly they will stick to passive aggressive comments.

One time whilst having a conversation with a full-blown overt narcissist, she was telling me how she does her shopping at all the *expensive places* and only eats at the nicest restaurants (*very superficial woman*). I told her that every so often I go to Waitrose (a nice supermarket chain in the UK) and buy a cheesecake for myself as a treat, and I asked her, "Have you tried their cheesecake?

It's incredible. I highly recommend it." Her response was, "You buy the WHOLE cheesecake?? All for yourself???" Clearly, my answer was, "Well, I don't eat it all in one go if that's what you're insinuating."

Another example with the same person I mentioned: I was popping out for a sandwich for lunch, and I came back 30 minutes later with the sandwich in a bag, but inside was a drink and a phone charger that I picked up from the store. She quipped, "That looks like more than just a sandwich!!" She was clearly insinuating that I was some sort of disgusting glutton.

These sound like petty comments, but they're perfect examples of passive aggressive bullying comments. If I reply, it exposes an insecurity; if I stay quiet, she wins with her bullying passive aggressiveness. The best thing to do is just to be quiet. Sadly, this sad pathetic woman has her own baggage, so I pray for her really.

Narcissistic rage will present itself in the 'not so public' situations, mostly when you are one-on-one with that person. Behind all the public facade is an evil, cold, shallow, superficial demon who wants to control, manipulate, and destroy lives. They want people to fall into the same dark endless hole they are in.

If a narcissist doesn't get their own way, if they feel 'betrayed', if they feel challenged – if you don't play by their rule book – you could see narcissistic rage. This will come in the form of physical violence or a demonic look that could make anyone quiver. They often call this 'the narcissistic stare'.

Narcissists are constantly acting as if they are on stage. Narcissistic rage is a deviation from this performance, to the point where they will literally spiral out of control. They will spin in a frenzy (often literally); they will pull their hair out; they will stomp around. It is almost like an adult baby throwing their toys out of an imaginary pram. All the above are literal examples; it's THAT ridiculous.

However, narcissistic rage is borderless and could lead to serious harm, even murder. Some of the most notorious killers were psychopathic, sociopathic narcissists. Of course, I'm saying the most extreme of examples, but it's a possibility. They have murder and violence within them.

## Mirroring

Mirroring is a technique narcissists, and toxic people in general, use to manipulate their targets. Often in society, people are very self absorbed. Their immediate focus is on themselves; what will they do today, what will they eat, where will they go, what will they buy; and then similarly, those actions are often shared onto their social media page: 'This is where I am', 'This is how I feel', 'This is what I think', 'This is what I'm doing' – sadly, most of society is a 'me' culture, and social media is the breeding ground for that.

One of the ways to spot a narcissist is, in fact, to notice their responses to what you say. You may tell them you have a holiday planned, and their response will be to tell you their experience of that holiday: "Oh, I've been there. I went there three years ago; I had a great time." Some may say this is conversation, and perhaps it is. But before they ask, "When are you going?" "Who are you going with?" "Are you excited?" they will respond with something about themselves.

Derren Brown, the world-famous psychologist and illusionist, actually mentions in one of his books that people are always talking about themselves, even if they don't realise it.

Narcissists do something called 'Mirroring', which plays up to this very character trait. They copy what you do. You may be talking to them, and they will shadow your body language, your mannerisms, the way you say things – and this builds a rapport. It's something best friends do subconsciously. People's accents will change to match that of the people closest to them. Their mannerisms and even, to some extent, their personality will change to fit in. Rapport building is an area all its own, but Narcissists do mirroring for manipulative reasons. They lack empathy and they do things to almost 'appear' human; this goes as far as actually mimicking people who they'd perceive as being 'normal'. They do this to build a rapport and have their targets connected to them.

It will feel like the ideal relationship. You'll have so much in common. The same tastes and interests, the same mannerisms, you will feel like long lost siblings or lovers who were meant to be.

It's all fake. In fact, what's happening is that you are falling in love with yourself. The narcissist will play this game with multiple people – they will be a different person to different people. You don't see this. You won't see how narcissists act around other people. They will go so far as to conceal that other persona, to make sure the rabbit doesn't get out of the hat. My ex narcissistic girlfriend never let me meet her friends or her family; in hindsight, it was because I knew she was someone else to them. I saw a picture of her once when she was out with friends. I didn't recognise the person. She looked completely different. I saw a text message of hers to someone else, and it was different to how she texted me. The way the words were written and the punctuation, it was like a different person.

Narcissists mirror you for several reasons.

1) To build a rapport and have you become very attached to them (you're really becoming attached to a version of yourself). This will allow the narcissist to get supply from you – and feel powerful from your attention.

2) To appear 'normal'. They don't have a base self; they don't have a personality, so they want to conceal this by simply mimicking or 'mirroring' you.

3) To build trust and have access to your inner most secrets. They never forget what is told to them, and they will use everything against you. Even the most subtle things will be stored, and months and years down the line, this information will be unleashed on you in an attempt to ridicule, embarrass, and shame you.

**Future Faking**

Future Faking is something narcissists do to control their target. When they get into a relationship, they want to create an illusion for their partner that they are here for the long term. If they find someone who they believe is co-dependent, future faking will work and have the person emotionally attached. It's essentially planning for a future together, often early in a relationship. Narcissists will want to get married; they will want to move in with you; they will plan how many kids they want and what their names will be. It's all very 'cute', but it is all lies. The co-dependent will absorb it; they are the hopeless romantic who will fall for it (many of us have been victim to it). Finally, you think, 'someone I can spend my life with'. Narcissists fake being the perfect soul mate, they're so convincing. But it's all a deception. They are the fallen angels of this world. They are completely fake. In fact, a relationship with them is never even a relationship. You're never fully on board with them. They will cancel on you; they won't introduce you to their friends or family. They will keep you at arms length. A relationship with a narcissist is a nonstarter. Be careful.

## Triangulation

Triangulation is a term used for when a narcissist is controlling the rhetoric, smear campaigning their target, dictating the next steps of the conversation, but in actuality is removed from the situation. The narcissist wants to cause trouble, but they don't want to be linked to the crime. To do this, they will use their 'minions' (aka Flying Monkeys).

Imagine the narcissist with a giant spoon stirring the waters, and whilst all the chaos is occurring around them, they sit there silently, sniggering to themselves, and no one suspects they are the cause of the chaos.

Narcissists are extremely manipulative people and triangulation is just another manipulation technique used to ensure they can cause harm without being directly responsible. Think of it like a Mafia boss, who arranges for their Under Boss (who is loyal through silence) to arrange for their runner (who is also sworn to secrecy) to arrange for their understudy to do a hit job on someone. There's a chain of command, with levels of secrecy which will remove the Mafia boss, the instigator of the whole thing, from any accusation.

# CHAPTER 1
# WHAT IS NARCISSISTIC ABUSE?

To begin, we need to understand and dissect what Narcissistic Abuse is. This is no easy feat; in fact, the term itself is somewhat 'man made', and it's not recognized by a court of law. It's a form of emotional abuse with long lasting damage; however, identifying it can be blurry and ambiguous.

Exploring the term will help us understand the journey we're embarking on to move away from the toxic relationships. In this book, you will hear me referring to narcissists and toxic people as mutually the same individuals, but note they can differ in personality traits – such as inhibiting sociopathic behaviours, psychopathic 'anti-social personality disorder' behaviours, etc.

Though we're exclusively talking about narcissists, the recovery tools in this book will work for any toxic individual or relationship.

**So, what is 'Narcissistic Abuse'?**
As complex as the topic is, I'd define Narcissistic Abuse as being the emotional pain, confusion and distress one feels after spending a systained period of time with someone who has Narcissistic Personality Disorder. Key symptoms can be, depression, lowered self esteem, lonliness, isolation, confusion, financial loss, paranoia and resentment. It's taken years of study to be able to summarise this complex area.

Narcissism and Narcissistic behaviours can be studied and discussed for countless hours. I have over nine hours of video blogs on my YouTube Channel, Aydin RD, discussing only this topic. However, there are a few key traits we can discuss to summarise the disorder.

Narcissists love themselves, but they also despise themselves. Complicated, I know. They believe in an ideal, perfect self, and they look to portray this to the world around them. However, the truth is, they are not perfect and they know this, but they can't handle that. They can't bear the thought of the World seeing an imperfection in them. This simple internal struggle is the eye of the storm and the tornado of chaos they inflict on others.

For an in-depth review of type of things Narcissists do, check out my e-book *Behind the Mask: An Introduction into Covert Narcissism*. You will get an idea for the tools they use: Gaslighting, Ghosting, Hoovering, Love Bombing, Blackmail, Manipulation, Smear Campaign, Lies, Rage, Confusion, the list goes on and on.

The Narcissist's crippling insecurity leads them down a dark path. Are they pathologically the way they are, or is it learned behaviour? In my opinion, it's both. The narcissist, at some point in their life, has experienced a life trauma, and as a result, has built walls around themselves, several defence mechanisms and 'survival traits'. They've also looked to create a fake self because they can't bear the reality of the real self.

Deep down, the narcissist is a lonely, boring, childish, undeveloped mess inside. Everything their life (and persona) is built on is a lie. It's fake, and at some point in their life, that fake life will become apparent – and the narcissist will fall apart. The mask will slip. They have no coping mechanisms.

The Narcissist will lie compulsively to maintain their 'perfect image'. They will always play the victim and deny wrongdoing and responsibility. They are jealous of others and extremely vengeful. They also hide their acts from the public eye – ensuring that 'perfect image'.

## What is 'Abuse'?

The English definition of 'abuse' is 'To treat with cruelty or violence, regularly or repeatedly'. There is no question that Domestic Abuse fits into this category. Abuse comes in several different ways. Physical violence, bullying, sexual and verbal attacks, beatings – it goes on and on. Though psychological abuse is important to note, too, and it's not a widely recognised area.

The Law likes to see 'bruises' or 'marks' as a sign of proof, solid evidence of the crime. A voice recording of the perpetrator caught in the act, for example. Abusers tend to hide their aggressive nature with a persona that most don't see. They have a public mask, so to speak. A great example of this is O.J Simpson. An admired, worshipped athlete-turned-movie star who was the face of Hertz and a sports broadcaster. However, he had a dark side, and as revealed in his court case in 1994, those domestic abuse allegations came to light with the recordings of Nicole Brown's 911 calls. As seen in the famous documentary *OJ: Made in America,* those closest to him and the jurors were shocked when they heard those tapes. One person from the show described it 'as if seeing a good person no longer be good'. Mark Furhman, a detective from the case, also commented on seeing OJ holding a baseball bat with rage-filled eyes and a vein popping from his forehead, with Nicole weeping on a smashed windscreen. This was the side of OJ no one saw. As with most abusers, it is very hidden, secluded, and disguised.

Unless there's a mark, unless there are tapes, it is very difficult to pin an abuser to the crime. This leads us to the next concept: proving the nature of abuse that narcissists will inflict on their targets. As the definition says, it's to treat another person with cruelty or violence – well, gaslighting is cruel. As defined in the glossary of terms on an earlier page, it's the purpose of misguiding a person to make them look a) stupid and b) question their sanity, which can lead to feelings of low self-esteem, confidence issues, and a plethora of mental issues. Another thing narcissists do is conduct smear campaigns, and they passive aggressively look to ruin the target's reputation. Is this cruel? Yes, it is.

The only issue with these examples are that they are very hard to prove. There are no video tapes; there are no marks. There is very little to pin to the perpetrator. It's an emotional feeling – something very difficult for a court to convict.

Narcissists hide in the shadows and attack from afar. They don't have the self-esteem to confront you. They would simply crumble under any confrontation and either i) charm their way out of the situation or ii) lie and deny any wrongdoing. They really are the weasels of society. They also like to attack you when they're around other people, and they'll do it in a 'joking' way – so that any reaction would present you as the sensitive one. It's all part of their plan: incriminate you, attack you, but avoid retaliation.

It's important not to lose hope. This book will provide a comprehensive guide on how to recover from your experience with a narcissist. There are tools I've personally used to get my life back which you can integrate into your own life to get your confidence and independence back.

It won't be easy, and it will take time. But I'm sharing the techniques and methods I personally used to get my life back and claw my way up from rock bottom – it worked for me, so I sincerely hope it works for you.

Now that we've established the meaning of Narcissism and Abuse in their simplest forms and looked at the techniques of abuse narcissists engage in via the Glossary of Terms, we can dig a bit deeper and get a basic overview of what this type of abuse looks like and how it affects the target.

# CHAPTER 2
## IMPACT OF ABUSE

How a person feels after being the target of a narcissist is unique to that individual. But I'm going to share with you how I felt, and perhaps you will identify with it.

Dealing with a narcissist is an un-winnable battle. An uphill walk in quicksand. A walk through a dark forest with no end. It's a hopeless, soul destroying feeling. Everything you say is scrutinized. Everything you do is judged and laughed at. Anything remotely empowering is shot down and ridiculed. Everywhere you go, you are judged and slandered. You can't move, think, sleep, or breathe without thinking of the narcissist. They burrow into your head, your soul, your psyche, and they don't let go. They weave into the veins of your very existence – to the point where you start to mimic them. They poison and corrupt good people.

They are the definition of evil. They dominate everything you do. They emotionally control you and make you feel guilty for making them feel 'sad', although you haven't done anything wrong – it is them, simply, ensuring you do not stay happy. They don't want you to be happy. Happiness and success to them is a threat. They want to be the centre of attention. And they are; one way or another, they are the ones being talked about.

This leads to an extremely hopeless feeling. You will start second guessing yourself. You will lose self esteem, confidence, you will become a shell of yourself. You have done everything and any-thing to grab positive attention from the narcissist, but it is to no avail. Literally nothing you can do will make them acknowledge or respect you. True evil does not know how to respect. They lack integrity.

You will lose your way in life. Your dreams will be shattered; friendships will be lost; your emotions will be unstable. Narcis-sists manipulate you in many ways, but one of the more unique ways is Love Bombing and then devaluing you. They will shower you will compliments. "I love you", "Your eyes are amazing", "You're so talented". If you end up dating them, they will want to get married quickly; they will want to move in quickly. They shower you with praise, admiration and 'love'. Then, they will drop you! Suddenly, they will drop you as quickly as last week's pizza. You will be nothing to them. A mere footnote. They won't meet you or speak to you, and they will completely ghost you.

One step worse, a narcissist will unleash a vicious smear cam-paign on you. After any argument, or notion of confrontation, they will humiliate you to their friends, your friends, and their close circle of people, also known as 'Flying Monkeys'. Narcissists are very charming people; they can manipulate people and have people eating out of their hands. These 'cronies' are known as Flying Monkeys and will often do the Narcissist's dirty work for them – spying on you, gathering information, ridiculing you. Any-thing to shunt your progress in life. Narcissists want to control you. And you will feel controlled. You will feel out-of-control with your own life. Everything you do will be dictated by the narcissist.

The damage can last years, potentially a lifetime. A narcissist can bully you, passively, covertly, and you wouldn't even notice it.

Good people expect others to also be good. But that's not how it works. Toxic people do exist. I have a family member, who in 31 years has never given me one single compliment. Actually, that's not true. This particular family member gave me one compliment about 12 years ago. I remember it vividly because it took me off guard. One compliment in 31 years.

This family member never asked me what I'd been up to or how my life was going. And if she did, when I'd reply, it'd be met with disgust. Let me give you an example.

"What have you been up to?" she'd ask.

"Oh, not much. I went to a concert the other night with a buddy, it was cool". The response from her would be a disgusted face and turning away in silence. She did not want to know. ZERO interest. Like I'd done something wrong. And that's just it. It's the same for all narcissists; they don't care. They don't want to care, they'd rather you be dead than the notion of you being happier than they are.

The bullying can last a lifetime, and when you realize what has been happening, you will kick yourself for not noticing it sooner. It's like a light-bulb moment. It's a liberating moment, because you can start getting your life back and building yourself again. That's what this book will help you do, re-build YOU.

I think this gives you the picture of what we're dealing with. I had it easy. I never had a child with a narcissist. I was able to get away. One of the tools I will be talking about is No Contact, and you will hear me mention a lot throughout this book. But some don't have that privilege of going 'no contact'. Having a child with a narcissist, having to see them, living under the same roof, potentially going through a divorce. These are nightmare scenarios.

And I will address ways to mitigate these situations to hopefully make your life easier and more comfortable. What you will read in the next chapters are 12 crucial life steps that you can take to start to rebuild, to take your life back and recover from the nightmare horror show that is narcissistic abuse.

# CHAPTER 3
## STEP ONE – REGAIN CONTROL OF YOUR LIFE

Look around you. Everything you absorb and consume has been purposely put there for its intended purpose. We are bombarded with marketing: buy this, look at this, visit here, wear these shoes! Celebrities have a major influence on this; their Instagram accounts are 'lifestyle' advertisements, showing people what a perfect, ideal life should look like. What would you do if you had all their millions?

Everything, down to the music we listen to, is controlled by a handful of corporations. Even the food we eat is controlled by a handful of stores. You can count them with one hand. The truth is, we don't have an awful lot of control in our lives. The same channels air the same shows pretty much every day. We are told what to watch. We are told what to listen to. We are told how to live.

Unless you let it. One of the main issues with narcissistic abuse is that you don't feel like you have any control, and in truth, you don't. Everything you say is scrutinized. Everything you do is judged. Everything you wear is ridiculed. Everything about you is laughed at – your clothes, your accent, your lifestyle, your job, your shoes, your hairstyle. Everything. Narcissists will fire at you with everything, all in a way that is difficult to defend. They won't compliment you; they won't acknowledge any success; they won't acknowledge anything good in you. It's incredibly draining. You have no control of that.

Add on to that the society we live in. Everything around us is carefully placed to encourage you to buy, to consume, to live by other people's rules; the task is very difficult. It's an uphill walk with a giant boulder attached to you.

I came to a point in my life where I felt I lost control of.my life and had nowhere to turn. I analysed the world we live in and realised that it's so easy to fall into a trap, especially when narcissists are around. We often don't realise people mean harm, but they do. Most people are out for themselves, even the Corporations; we live in shark-infested waters, and the trouble is, they are everywhere!

My light bulb moment came when I was driving to work one day. My daily commute involved listening to the radio – BBC 1 Radio to be specific. And depending on what time I was going to work, a specific DJ would be hosting the show at that time. I don't want to mention names, but a few of the DJs made me completely miserable. They spoke about 'pop culture', 'current news' and played the same songs that have been circulating for the past two years. I was miserable, and I didn't even really realise it. I was consuming this information on a daily basis, not realizing that it's just another aspect of my life where I appear to have no control. For years, I've been listening to the same mindless drivel, the same jokes, the same schtick, the same music and, in conclusion, I realised I can control this. I can regain control of this aspect of my life. I turned the radio off. I drove in silence.

That was two years ago (from the time of writing this). I haven't turned the radio on since. I have glanced at the Top 40 music charts to see if I'd missed anything. I hadn't. It was all the same names. The same people releasing the same crap; I hadn't missed a thing.

In that time, I've chosen what to listen to: my own music track lists, podcasts, interesting videos on YouTube; though such a small thing, I have regained control of the information I consume through media. No longer are these mindless DJs polluting my mind. My mind was already destroyed and polluted; I was miserable and recovering from a sequence of nightmare relationships.

I went a step further and decided to analyse the TV I was watching. The same people, every day, were speaking to me about the same shows.

"Did you watch this?"

"Oh, my! Did THAT just happen?"

"How did they kill all the characters!?"

The same people, talking about the same shows. I knew I had lost control. I looked at my viewing habits, and observed that I was watching…nothing. I technically *was* watching something, but it wasn't anything significant. Just the news, some documentaries, the games. But I questioned whether I should be watching the same things as everyone else? We are literally socially engineered to like certain things. Now, don't get me wrong, I like *Game of Thrones*. It's an interesting show. But it's not THAT good! It's not. To be perfectly honest, I don't even know what happens half the time. I liked *Breaking Bad*; that was a cool show. But I haven't seen *The Walking Dead*, or *Prison Break*, or *House of Cards*. I'm sure they're great shows, but I'm made to feel like an alien for not knowing about them.

I took action. I turned off the TV. I cancelled my subscriptions. This was a difficult thing for me to do. I didn't think I could cope (as sad as that sounds). But it's been 1 year! And I feel great. I haven't missed a single thing. I watch the games at the local bar, socialise a bit more. I watch things on YouTube, and I've recently purchased Netflix. I don't need TV. I don't need people telling me what to watch and when to watch it. The only thing that ever made me happy on TV was *The Sopranos*, and that was years ago. It was maybe the best show ever made; I legitimately looked forward to each episode. Since then, I can't think of anything else that caught my interest.

You need to gain control of your life. What are the things you don't have control over, that need to be enforced a bit more? Feel empowered again to do the things you like and to consume the things you want. We got to rock bottom by feeling out of control, so you can make some easy decisions to regain some of that control.

If we let the system consume us, even our time is controlled. We'd be like robots: Work 9-5; come home tired; have a weekend; go out on the weekend; be hungover on Sunday. REPEAT. You have power to break that cycle. Go out on a Tuesday. Go out on a Monday! Do something different to break the chain. Repetition is a disease; you will lose yourself in repetition and monotonous cycles.

Even the food you eat should be analysed. Are you eating the same things from the same places? Well, change it. Go somewhere different; try something new. Break the norm. Try some of the indie food stores; support local stores. Try cooking something different. Don't let the system control you.

Social media is a real hotbed for control, and again, it's simply that we're fed what to see and believe. In recent times, we've heard about the lion who was brutally murdered by the dentist. That's a tragic event, and it caused an uproar (no pun intended). However, sadly, that kind of thing happens regularly. Animals, not just lions, are inhumanely slaughtered every day. It's a shocking fact. I saw online that a giraffe was giving birth, and most of my social media was commenting on the giraffe. A giraffe, giving birth. Yes. This ignited passion in people. Why? Someone somewhere put a live stream of the giraffe, and it caught fire. However, this happens every day. Animals give birth; humans give birth. It's how species survive.

It's time to regain some control. It's all right to micromanage your life in some areas, but don't become crazy with it. It's all right to be a bit selfish and focus on yourself. A healthy, strong-minded YOU is better for everyone. Just look at some of the main things you consume and try to change them. The radio, the TV, the social media – we're bombarded but don't let it get to you. Look at your life cycle, your Monday-to-Friday routine and try to change it. YOU decide what you want to see and hear. YOU decide what you want to consume. YOU have more control than you think. This is an important first step in you finding yourself again.

We are here to rebuild. We are here to start again. When you're at rock bottom, you need to build from the ground up. So, let's clean out the closet, let's get rid of the old clothes (metaphorically), and let's rebuild a new YOU.

# CHAPTER 4
## STEP TWO – LET GO OF THE PAST

Narcissistic abuse is an incredibly traumatic experience. You have been bullied, lied to, deceived, embarrassed, made a fool of, bankrupted, lied about and tricked. You've been scarred. Someone, through their own self hatred, jealousy, and agenda has sought to destroy you, to lower your self esteem, to ruin your reputation.

It's a lot to take in; it's often ambiguous and confusing. You might not know it's happening. Narcissists are incredibly deceptive people. You may even question whether you've done something wrong, which compounds the confusion. However way you cut and slice it, one of the reactions is clear: to get revenge, to fight back, and to make them pay. These are all normal reactions. I've said it several times, narcissists corrupt good people.

You will have an urge to make them pay, and this will consume you. All along, the narcissist will sit back and use their flying monkeys to get you. The monkeys will spy on you, lie to you, gather information on you, and relay that material back to the narcissist. The flying monkeys' whole agendas are to 'play along' with the narcissist's games. The monkey may see the narcissist as being in a position of power that can help them, or perhaps the narcissist has something the monkey wants. A female narcissist will often use the lure of sex to keep someone close.

You find yourself in this position of being attacked, deceived, and embarrassed, and you want to fight back. Whilst doing that, you have a gang of minions secretly plotting against you, and an extremely toxic narcissist in the middle of it all, with various walls around them. They are extremely difficult to get a hold of, and in some cases identify.

This will consume you. These feelings you're having will consume you. I appreciate if you're going through a divorce, or through court, or have children with a narcissist, things will get very difficult (and that's an understatement). If you have narcissistic parents, this will compound the confusion. You will have feelings of guilt and regret due to the divine unconditional love-rights most parents have (and that's another issue). You may even work with a person causing you these traumas. It's not easy to walk away from, but you MUST walk away. This is also known as going NO CONTACT.

There's a technique that publicists use for their clients when a huge story comes out. Whether it's a sex tape, a scandal, or troubling news that will damage the celebrity's reputation, a publicist really earns their money in situations like these. They have a technique I've noticed used in several of these situations, and it's called, 'Going Dark'. No, this is not spending a few hours on the sunbed, this is a technique whereby you go completely silent. No social media posts, no text messages, no phone calls, no public appearances – you go 'dark'. You do this for several months, maybe four to six months. You go quiet.

The World we live in goes so fast that within weeks, a new story will take over people's minds. As mentioned in the previous chapter, one day it's a lion, the next it's a giraffe, a gorilla, etcetera. It goes on and on, and things get forgotten. Society consumes so much information. Whatever is going on in your world, a four- to six-month silent treatment will help a lot. Those Flying Monkeys, that smear campaign, that issue that was the talk of the town, will be largely forgotten, but not completely.

I've been no contact with a family member for almost two years now, and sadly, I can still count on one hand the times I've had to be in the same room as them. There are going to be times when you need to be in the same room. Going No Contact is not easy. One thing I struggled with is narcissists don't evolve, so their perception of you won't either, even if you have changed. Narcissists are just a black hole of destruction. They consume, they corrupt, and they spit people out. They don't grow and evolve themselves. That's not who they are. They live in a make-believe reality, and it's only the illusion that changes for them. The thing I struggled with was, even if one year goes by, I know the narcissist is still going to perceive me as they once did 5-10 years ago. And it's true! They will. You need to accept this. Even if in that time, for example, you became a CEO of your own company, an owner of a charity that helped millions, married a beautiful woman and had kids and a beautiful home – the narcissist won't recognise any of that. They will just see you how they used to see you. They don't evolve. Don't expect them to.

Going Dark is a great way to calm waters but going No Contact is your long-term solution for recovering from the traumas and attacks of a Narcissist.

You need to let go of the past. Those feelings of revenge need to go, and you need to walk away. This doesn't only include the target; you need a complete refresh of the people you thought you knew. Part of recovering means gaining control, and sometimes to do that you need to be ruthless. My recommendation would be anyone associated with the narcissist needs to be grouped into the same category as the narcissist. Go No Contact from them, too. Any friend of theirs, any ex-girlfriend, anyone with whom they may have had a relationship, anyone you see hanging out with them. Remove them from your social media, remove their phone numbers (if you have them). Don't associate with THEM.

I must reiterate that this is not going to be easy. If you work in the same place, or if it's a family member, of course there are going to be exceptions. However, within reason, you need to cut contact with anyone associated with the narcissist.

I did this, and it wasn't easy. I had 'friends' text messaging me, asking why I deleted them from Facebook, why I haven't been responding to them. There are several ways in which I could have responded, but I knew these same people were talking bad about me and gossiping about me with the narcissist.

If you need to question who your friends are, who loves you and who is loyal to you, and vice versa, then they most probably are not those things. You shouldn't have to question it. Life is too short to waste on people who are 'temporary'. You will know who your lifetime friends are; and often, you can count them with one hand. They are the people who are there for you, who care for you, and who want you to do well in life. The others – they can fall by the way side.

Letting go of the past is not going to be easy if you have children with the narcissist. In these situations, you need to dramatically reduce contact where possible. You should be cutting contact with any mutual friends, with no reason given. Basically, if they're associating with the person who has hurt you beyond belief, then they should be coupled into that same category. A true friend will understand the harm the narcissist has caused and will not associate with them.

If the narcissist is a family member, go No Contact with the understanding that associating siblings might be difficult. Family is family, but if someone causes you harm, be ruthless and cut that contact. This boils down to setting strong boundaries for yourself. What are your rules? What are the guidelines for people when they speak with you? If someone disrespects you and disrespects your privacy and integrity, are you going to let them get away with it? It doesn't matter if they are family or not, these boundaries need to be established, and you need to stick to them.

Family members often believe they have a divine right to know everything about you. Then they betray your trust and share your private conversations to others. Why? Why do they do that? It's because they don't think you will ever go away. Family is family, right? Well, that can change. And though I'd recommend going No Contact with family with caution, it shouldn't be taken off the cards completely.

You are your own spiritual being, with boundaries, with integrity, with self respect. No one on this planet should betray that. No one. If you extend the same courtesy to others, and they should do the same for you. It's all about respect. And sometimes, family members betray that.

Letting go of the past will allow you to move forward. Imagine the past as a huge weight attached to you by a steel chain. You're trying to soar like an eagle; you're trying to run free, the fresh air of life hitting your face, but this weight is slowing you down; it's causing you pain. You're walking slowly, step by step, with anguish on your face, but that past is still there, and it's stopping you. You need to cut free. That weight, that bolder that represents your past needs to be cut off. This will allow you to start running, to start soaring, to embrace a new life with new things to explore, new ventures you never knew were possible. You can soar through life, fearlessly, building a new future for yourself, taking on new ground and evolving in a way the narcissist could never evolve.

Imagine two trees side by side. One of them is your past; the other is your future. Your past is, in terms of size, bigger than your future because your future hasn't happened yet. It's all potential. Now, for a tree to grow, it needs sunlight. Sunlight will help the tree grow. Now imagine your future tree is in the shadow of the past. The sunlight is unable to get to your future tree because the past is hovering over it, stunting your growth. You need to cut the past tree and allow the sunlight to get to your future. It's a strange analysis, but it's true. Don't let the past stunt the growth of your future. Cut that tree away; move on from your past; cut it down; put it aside and move on. You will grow as a human; be fearless and let it happen. You are more incredible than you will ever know. Letting go is an important first step. The end is the best beginning.

# CHAPTER 5
## STEP THREE – TRUST YOUR GUT INSTINCT

Always trust your gut instinct. We live in a world where the majority of people wish for your downfall. They won't want you to get that promotion; they don't want you to get that new home; they don't want your business to be successful. But that's ok. That's just a cold, hard, fact of life. Society has made the human race into somewhat of a rat-race.

"Here is the promised land; this is what HAPPY looks like", and they wave these products, these cars, these celebrities with crispy fresh clothes and luxurious nightclubs with $1000 bottles of booze. Is that what happiness is? I guess it's not completely depressing, but there's more to it. People gauge their own success by how big their TV is, or how big their home is, and how much they earn. This mentality leads to one thing: most people want you to fail, they don't want you to have better things than them or to be more 'successful' than them.

If you meet someone who wishes you well, value them. They are good people. When I wrote my book The Devil In I, it helped me open my eyes to the people in my life who were genuine. Some people close to me never mentioned it, never asked about it. However, some people in my life were incredibly supportive. For this, I'll never forget them and will always be a friend to each of them. Sometimes you need these eye openers to help you realise who the important people are in your life.

I digress. The whole idea of most people wanting you to fail leads to my key point in this chapter. People will purposely give you advice that is secretly designed to hurt you.

"Don't go for that job, because you could struggle, crash and burn, and you'll be depressed."

"Don't go for that investment, you could lose it all."

"That girl who you think is the girl of your dreams, she's not all that. She's a gold digger, and you can do much better!"

These are all things I've personally heard. This advice has harmed me. In hindsight, I can see it was designed to confuse me, to keep me down, and to ensure I don't thrive in my life.

Facebook had launched an IPO and was offering shares, if my memory serves me, I believe it opened at $18 a share. It may have been a few bucks higher or lower. In short, I felt there was some potential with this. I was new to investing and was fairly nervous about it, but I analysed it, and I believed, with the user base of Facebook, and how integrated it is into the Internet, with the share options on every website, Instagram, and incredible revenues – I felt that the IPO offering was generous.

My gut instinct was telling me to invest. I thought it could be as successful and valuable as Google one day. Before I pulled the trigger, I reached out to someone I trusted to get a second opinion.

"This is a waste of time stock", I was told, "This is a rich man's stock, only rich people should invest in this stock This is not your business", I was informed.

"Don't get involved in things you don't know. You will lose all your money".

This was the advice I was given. It confused me. It made me doubt myself, even though my own logic and intuition told me otherwise. I didn't invest.

Facebook stock, at this point as I write this, is $150 a share. That's over 7x more than the original offering. My life savings would have increased 7 times over. SEVEN.

I learnt a valuable lesson that day and today: Always trust your gut instinct. People don't want you to increase your portfolio by seven times. They don't. Why would they? Why would they want you to do something they haven't done?

Most people want you to be lower than they are. Lesser than them and forever struggling.

Trust your gut instinct. One thing I will always teach my son is, never be afraid to take risks. Don't be afraid of making mistakes. Life is a game. You will win, you will lose, but you need to participate. You need to be 'in it to win it' so to speak.

This same mindset of trusting your intuition extends to narcissists. Your body and your soul will tell you when something is wrong. We have millions of years of evolution teaching us "fight or flight." Humans once survived in the wild, without any extraordinary physical skillsets. We can't run very fast; we can't climb too well; we're not extraordinarily strong, yet in the wild we survived. There are several reasons for that survival, but one of them is our intuition, which has been honed and developed, evolving for centuries. Trust it.

I remember several years ago, a new person entered the workplace. I always give people the benefit of the doubt and never want to judge people based on what I've heard until I've spoken to them a few times. I think that's the best way to live life. However, as bizarre as it sounds, this new person was like a B-movie actor. This person was playing the role of a 'humble, mature, salt of the earth guy', and the acting was so off; think of a terrible movie you'd see in the bargain basket at Walmart for $1. Just terrible. It was so contrived. I instantly had a bad feeling about this person.

To be honest, I didn't even have a reason to dislike this guy. He had done nothing to me. I didn't even really know who he was; my opinion and mindset didn't even matter. But, immediately, that first day, my intuition was telling me to watch out. I didn't know why until years afterward.

Years later, this person was found to be a workplace bully. He'd make impressions of people, making fun of them. He'd ridicule positive people. He made sideways swipes about me and some of my business ventures, and even my home. I knew, then, that this person was bad news. Going back through all those years – I had known it from the very first day. It's sad when someone is so insecure, whether because of the way they look or their broken home, or just their position in life, that they need to strike out at others in a covert passive-aggressive way. It's a pity.

If you get a weird feeling that someone is sneaky, ingenuine, agenda driven, and extremely insecure – then they most probably are. You should never have to question someone's motives; if you need to question it, there's a reason for it.

# CHAPTER 6
## STEP FOUR – FIND YOUR VICE / FIND YOUR PURPOSE IN LIFE

I remember I had just left college. I earned a degree in International Politics and was quite hopeful for the future. I had my career path set out; I was planning to stay at home for a few months before venturing into the post-college 'real' world. I was hopeful. I was happy. It was going to be an exciting new start in my life.

My dream was always to be in a band. That was my purpose. I had been playing guitar since I was a kid, and my dream was to make it as a professional musician. That was my purpose in life; it's what I was working towards and I was content with that. I was comfortable with that mission, I woke up every day and my goal was to somehow make it as a professional musician. Being with my band, being in a rehearsal room, or recording music was the most enjoyable thing to me. I could spend hours, and often did, in a studio making music fuelled on nothing but Red Bull. Add to that the feeling you get when performing a gig, even if it's to 10 people, was incredible. That's what I wanted to do with my life.

This dream was met with laughter and ridicule. Note what I said about 'the majority of people wanting you to fail'. It was no different in this case. My dreams did not make sense to people who were assimilated to the standard ideals of what a 'normal' life should be.

"You're living in dream land", they said. "No one makes it". "Go to work and get a real job".

Almost everyone I knew made me feel inferior for having this dream. There were no words of encouragement, "How shall we get there; what can I do to help?"

My whole idea was to give things a shot, and if they didn't work, I could move on and try something else. We only live once. But I was seen as a joke.

I gave my band a real shot and wanted see if it could go anywhere. We released an album and gave it a real push. The process was fun, but unfortunately, it didn't work out.

Whenever you a dependent on three other people to make your dreams work, it won't end well. Everyone needs to be on the same page, and sadly, in that time of my life, the other guys didn't share my viewpoints. One guy didn't want to leave his job to tour, the other was just starting a family, and generally, the overall commitment wasn't there to make it work. My dream, my purpose, my reputation had fallen to an all-time low. That was my purpose in life. My mission. And it was gone.

I spiralled into a deep depression. My family thought I was a bum. My friends didn't understand why I'd dedicated so much to making the band work. My siblings laughed at my ambitions. I was depressed, lonely, misunderstood. I no longer had a mission. I felt lost and lonely.

I isolated myself from society until I figured out what my new mission was going to be. I didn't want to let go. I figured, 'I can play guitar. Maybe I should look to be a session musician.'

I then decided to apply to a prestigious music college in Los Angeles. It's on Hollywood Boulevard – Musicians Institute. I applied and had to go through several examinations to be considered. I had to play several scales in various octaves and different styles of music. I even had to make a voice recording and explain why I wanted to go to Musicians Institute. I was so excited. After waiting several weeks, I got an email from the college. I had been accepted!

My dream of being a professional musician had a glimmer of hope! I thought of the networking I'd have in LA: the people I'd meet, the contacts I'd make, and the experience I'd have from being in that college. For the first time in years, I was feeling hopeful. My life mission was starting to formulate.

During this time, people were telling me I was stupid, and 'there's no money in music', that, 'I'd be away from family' and that 'no one makes it from that college'. Remember, people want you to fail!

However, I stayed focused and considered the offer. I got the details through, and the college threw the price tag at me. It was close to $100,000 just for the course. That didn't include the three years of accommodations required and living costs, which would have increased the budget to at least $200,000. I didn't have $200,000. I had to decline the offer.

I was back to square one. I decided to give up on my mission in life until further notice. During this time, family members made fun of me. Relatives said I was lazy. No one understood.

In short, I had lost my purpose and was completely depressed about it. YOU have to ask yourself, what is your purpose in life? Is it to work 9-5, and then go home and Snapchat every day about where you are and what you're drinking and eating? Is it to have the best car in your neighbourhood? Is it to have the biggest house in your village?

What is it? What do you live for? I often ask my friends what they want from life – and they can't answer me. They have no purpose. Whether you want to be a fireman, an actor, a musician, or a philanthropist, whatever it may be, in my opinion, people need that purpose. Even if your purpose is to be the best parent you can be – that's a great purpose. If you're reading this now, I'd like you to answer these three questions: What is your purpose in life? What is your goal? What is it you are trying to achieve?

The common answer, I'd assume, is 'to get rich'. Another friend of mine told me his life mission was to 'be a millionaire by the age of 30' and when I asked him how he was going to do that, he replied, 'I'm not sure'. Well, we'd all like to be millionaires, I'm sure, but at least flesh out a plan on how you're going to get there! How can something happen with no plan?

In my opinion, depression, insecurity, and low self-esteem come from, partly, a lack of life purpose. A lack of meaning. It's important to create one.

Get a piece of paper, or a huge whiteboard, a marker pen and start brainstorming. What is your mission statement, and how will you get there? It takes time; things happen step-by-step, so don't be afraid to checkpoint your progress into several sections. Rome wasn't built in a day, so they say.

Once you have achieved one part of it, move on to the next. A first goal could be to set up a company. Have a logo. A marketing plan. It could be to be a professional weight lifter, so go to the gym two to three times a week as a starting point. It doesn't matter how big or small the goal or purpose is, having one will bring you joy. It will bring meaning to your life.

One of the effects of narcissistic abuse is losing that meaning in your life. You may have spent years with the wrong person, been co-dependent on them, only for it to be thrown back in your face as one big lie. Feelings of loneliness and helplessness seep through into your soul.

Everything a narcissist says is one big lie, and their future faking is a key part of this. They will create this illusion of a perfect world – marriage, kids, a big home. Narcissists often create the illusion that they are incredibly wealthy people who can offer the world to you. The truth is, they are probably in mountains of debt by trying to create that image. Their life is one big lie.

Spotting a narcissist isn't an easy thing to do. Often it will take years to realise the person in your life wishes ill on you instead of good and isn't the emotionally secure person you once thought. It's insulting; it's embarrassing, and it requires you to rebuild.

Don't be afraid to rebuild. After narcissistic abuse, your reputation, your personality, your confidence, will all be in tatters. Narcissists use smear campaigns to manipulate the people around them, often their flying monkeys, to ensure they all have the same negative opinion of you.

Narcissists use gaslighting to make you feel like the crazy one. You will start to think you are insane.

An ex-narcissist of mine, a completely despicable individual, has a habit of dating married men (aka she's a homewrecker). On each occasion, I've heard stories of how the man had gone insane to the point of 'stalking' her, of coming to the house in the night, of messaging nonstop and threatening the family. It's a pattern I've heard several times, but I can't help but think what had happened to tip this person over the edge? I've heard of it with different individuals, and the 'victim' (aka, the accuser) is what I'd diagnose as a person suffering from narcissistic personality disorder.

The moral of this is, a narcissist will tip you over the edge. I'd never condone violent or threatening behaviour. But I'm also aware that a narcissistic, fake, image-conscious individual behind closed doors is capable of corrupting the nicest of people. Tipping them over the edge.

Be conscious of this. Narcissists will make you feel crazy and insane. Don't let them.

When you're at rock bottom. When you've lost your purpose in life. When you have no mission statement. You need to rebuild and create one. Trust me, I've been there.

You need to rebuild and recreate yourself. It's not always the easiest thing to do; you will feel like clinging to your previous goals, but sometimes moving on is the best way. Never give up, but be aware there is a time you will be flogging a dead horse.

One way to rebuild is to have a new life purpose, but another way leads nicely to my next point.

# CHAPTER 7
## STEP FIVE – CHOOSE YOUR FRIENDS WISELY / GO NO CONTACT IF YOU NEED TO

I saw a meme on Instagram the other day, which perfectly ties in to this point. It said, 'Life Is Too Short for Temporary People'. This is as true as it gets. Imagine the opposite, that you live your life with people who you know are not going to be there for you in 10 years' time.

We as people, friendly people, are far too accommodating. Just because you go to the same gym as someone, or work in the same place, or have mutual friends, it doesn't mean you need to be their friend. They can call you a friend, but the line between friend and acquaintance needs to be clearer. I've been guilty of being accommodating and friendly to everyone. It's not a bad trait, but sometimes I've blurred the lines between who is my actual friend and who is only a passer-by, a temporary person, so to speak.

I fell into the trap of letting narcissists into my home. If they don't see gold-plated jewels and furniture of the quality of royalty, they will find a way to ridicule it. If they have a bigger TV than you, they will smugly chuckle at it. They are the worst people to bring to your home. On this particular occasion, these two narcissists came as part of a party, and they had mutual friends. I was left in an unfortunate, difficult situation – they wanted to attend, and if I had said no, it would have looked bad to our mutual friends and perhaps soured the relationship. The very fact I thought of that was a mistake. I should have been more ruthless, and just said no.

Their turning up to the party lead to me being the brunt of a smear campaign. I didn't identify the issue until I was forced to go on holiday with one of these narcissists. Again, we shared mutual friends; on the holiday, he started talking about my previous business ventures – things I didn't realise he had any idea of. He started making fun of them. I knew then he had been stalking me. He also mentioned other things that I'd never discussed with him. It became apparent to me then narcissist had reared its head. It went a step further, and he secretly recorded me telling a story to the guys – typical locker room talk that one has when on vacation with friends.

These are the dangers with associating with people who a) pretend to be your friend and b) acquaintances, mutual friends of your real friends. You must be extremely careful these days. Remember what we mentioned in the previous chapter? People want you to fail. The majority of people want you to fail. Even some parents, to a degree, will distance themselves from you if they feel you may be more successful than they are. Most people don't want you to succeed and thrive in life.

I want you to do an exercise right now. I want you to get a piece of paper, whiteboard and marker pen, and list all your friends and family. All of them. Every single one.

Now, when you have your list, I want you to go through each name and put T or L next to it. T stands for Temporary and L stands for Lifetime. Will this person be there for you in 10 years' time? Will this person be there for you if you needed help? Does this person encourage you and inspire you to be a better person? Do you want to help this person? Are you there for this person whenever they need you?

By following those questions, it should be quite apparent who is temporary and who is lifetime. Sadly, the Lifetime list is going to be a lot smaller than the temporary list. It's important to know the difference.

Now that you have sight of the people in your life, you need to make the choice of moving forward in your life without them. I can't advise you to do anything, but I personally have removed 90% of the 'temporary' people in my life, and I'm so much happier for it.

I don't have to worry what people are saying behind my back. I don't have to worry about getting acceptance from someone. I don't have to worry about whether someone likes me or not. I've made that decision, and I know the people in my life right now are the lifetimers. Ok, there are some temporaries whose company I don't mind, but on the whole, it's lifetime people.

Even family members have got the cut. Remember I told you I was unemployed, depressed, and had lost my life purpose? Well, certain family members, siblings, friends of my mum, and other relatives all had something to say about me – I'm lazy; I'm deluded; I can't do anything; I won't amount to anything. The list goes on and on. People love to kick others when they are down, when they are rock bottom, but when you rebuild and rise from the ashes, they stay quiet.

I won't even let those people lace up my shoelaces now. I may say hello in passing, but they are nothing to me. I've made that choice and can differentiate between the important people in my life and the fakers.

In the context of narcissists, the only true way, in my opinion, to recover from narcissistic abuse is to go No Contact. You can't negotiate or rationalize with these people, they are way too manipulative. As the phrase goes, it's like wrestling with a pig; you'll get dirty, but the pig will love it. They love chaos; they love ruining lives; they love being the controller and manipulator of other people's emotions.

You must go No Contact, but that isn't always going to be easy, especially if it's a family member, or someone you work with, or someone you're getting divorced from. No Contact has its challenges.

I made a video on YouTube titled, 'How to Destroy A Narcissist'. It's slightly controversial because I make points, slightly ironic, on how to pander to them. Things such as, 'Don't ask them for anything', and, 'Always compliment them'. This sounds crazy, but in actuality, you're removing the nerve from them when purposely doing these things. You're removing their playbook, and they are going to get confused. These type of techniques should be used with caution and is ideally for situations when you can't go No Contact.

Going No Contact from the narcissist is one thing, but you also need to consider the people around the narcissist. Personally, I made a choice to disassociate with anyone close to the narcissist. I had certain rules I'd stick to. For example, if I saw someone post a picture on social media with the narcissist, I'd block that person and delete their number. Ruthless, I know, but why should I have a 'temporary' person in my life who is friends with a narcissist who looks to destroy me covertly? It's like the Vice President of the USA being seen having drinks with Vladamir Putin. It's exactly like that. Don't put up with it; make sure the people in your life are your close aides who want the best for you, and that feeling should be mutual.

Analyse and review the people close to the narcissist. Check on your list to see if someone is closely tied to the narcissist. If they tag themselves at the cinema, or a bar, or take photos together, that's a 'closer than a work colleague' link, and they should go. If you don't do this, the risk is they are a flying monkey and will report gossip back to the narcissist. Remember, narcissists use flying monkeys, people close to them who are also close to you, to gather information on you and spread gossip. The smear campaign and reputation damage are key weapons narcissists like to use.

The irony is that the narcissists often have the worst reputation of all, possibly promiscuous, drug-taking losers. Sadly, no one is manipulative and sad enough to try to destroy them in turn. There's a real trend with these narcissists, and they're mostly all the same. It's pitiful.

To summarise, we have a list of the temporary people, the lifetime people, and the people associated to the narcissist. You need to make decisions without worrying about mutual friends and associations; you need to decide whether you are going to block their social media profiles and remove their numbers.

We're rebuilding; we're building a stronger you. How can you move forward when you have these people in your life? These question marks will hover over your head as you try to build a new life for yourself. Do you really want these people gossiping about you? Doubting you? Telling you how wrong you are?

Narcissists, in some way, shape, or form, never leave your life. They always come back in some capacity. If you've ever dated one, you know this. They never disappear. They might go away for a year or two, but they do come back. You can't get away from them, so it's important for you to control what you can and make sure the people in your life are the loyal lifetimers with whom you can build a strong, happy future.

# CHAPTER 8
## STEP SIX – RESEARCH THE TOPIC OF NARCISSISM

Years may go by, and you will not realise that over time, you have been slowly bullied and drained of all your self-esteem and confidence by people near to you. Your family, friends, colleagues, lovers, teachers are all suspects. Narcissism is a psychological disorder which can affect anyone. The argument is still out there as to whether it is a pathological disorder or a product of one's environment and life situation that has led them down this path. The fact is, people are insecure; people are jealous and to compensate for that, they create a false sense of being – an unrealistic ascension of one's self; they literally become the King or Queen of their universe. On the surface, that doesn't sound like a bad thing; I'm a huge advocate of controlling your own destiny and feeling empowered to progress through life with confidence and ambition. However, it's important to do that with a healthy mind, a mind which is supportive of others.

Perhaps society has created a culture where the competition for validity is amplified by social media. How many followers and likes do you have? What cool restaurants and clubs you are in? What car you drive? What shows you watch? People, sadly, get caught up in that pressure to 'impress'; they forget about the reality. I saw a meme that comically summarised this issue. It said something like, 'Don't go broke trying to look rich. Act your wage'.

One of the coolest things I've seen was with a good friend of mine who owns an airline company. He is a very successful man, but you would never think it. He wears jeans, brandless t-shirt's and drives a modest car. Mark Zuckerberg is an example of that, too; he is very modest in how he dresses. I think that's cooler than all the 'bling' and glamour of trying to look 'rich' and important.

Anyhow, back to my original point about being confident with a healthy mind. It is a real mark of a person to see how they treat others who are doing well in life. When I first became an author, and I'll be honest, it was never a life plan of mine, it all came as a surprise. I noticed a lot of people around me changed. They lent away, whilst people who I didn't realise was close to me, showed incredible support. Through this journey of growth and discovery (and researching narcissism), I noticed unusual traits in the people around me, people who I thought were my friend. This equipped me to deal with it better and manage my own expectations of those people.

When The Devil In I came out, it received really good reviews. I was amazed and so humbled by this. I didn't think anyone would be interested in hearing about a story of a young Wall Street worker who is secretly The Devil. But, it surprised me and the reception was great.

On a personal level, many people were supportive. People with whom I hadn't spoken for years supported me, read the book, and said how amazing it was; they 'couldn't put it down'. Colleagues of mine, old high school friends, my best friend and their wives. It was extremely humbling, and it helped me see a side of them that I hadn't realised. Since then, those people, I value them as real friends. I will forever remember the support they showed me during that time.

However, there were other people whom I considered to be 'best friends' (they're obviously not) who still to this day have not asked me about the book. Have not read the book and have not done anything to support me through it. I have family members who still haven't read the book, and one particular narcissist, who has been the subject of several of my YouTube videos, has never even mentioned it to me.

The point I'm trying to make is, after researching and understanding narcissism, I understand why they would not read it, or why they would not be interested in asking me about it. I don't expect it from them

I sometimes wonder, if a family member or close friend wrote a book or did something like that, I'd willingly check it out. Even if I didn't read it all, I'd scan through it and ask if there's anything I can do to support them. I'd happily do that. But I'm not a narcissist. I'm not jealous, shallow, and insecure. I have pillars of integrity and self-respect on which I build my values. I can confidently support someone else's success without feeling my own journey is undermined. Narcissists, and people suffering from NPD, don't have those pillars. They are incapable of supporting someone who is 'doing well'. In fact, they'd lurk in the shadows and wait for you to fail, they'd then be the first to 'point and laugh'.

Since the release of The Devil In I, I can ascertain who the toxic people are in my life based on that one experience over one year. This allows me to manage my own expectations of those people. You must do the same.

Research the topic of narcissism, read as much as you can, watch as many YouTube videos as you can. Learn and cross reference everything. Then, apply it to your real-life experiences. You will be surprised to see that most people have narcissistic traits. It's a spectrum. People move along that spectrum in varying degrees. You may see someone act up in an overt way, or a covert way, or conduct themselves in an uncharacteristic manner that stunned you. This will then give you an insight into how they are feeling at that stage in their life.

There was a time I asked a family member, "If you could improve anything in your life, what would you improve?" Her reaction shocked me to the core. She looked at me with disgust and refused to answer.

"What sort of a question is that?" she quipped.

"Well, it's something I've been doing with myself, to try and figure out my knowledge gaps. I just want to be a better person," I replied.

"What a stupid exercise; it sounds so fake and contrived. Get real," she replied, with a disgusted look on her face.

I'd never seen anything like it. Then I realised, narcissists don't believe they can improve. Oddly, deep inside they are completely broken, but their surface persona should be, in their eyes, 'perfect'. To you, they will never disclose anything that needs improving. According to their script, their fake persona, they don't need improving.

That right there is an example of how my experience in studying narcissism allowed me to understand why a narcissist would reply in that way. I find joy in predetermining the outcome of someone's reaction. Narcissists are fake; they are not real. They are shells, make believe shells that pretend to be human. There are clear patterns used, and you'll be surprised how consistent these patterns are.

My ex-narcissistic girlfriend came out of the woodwork after two years. Interestingly enough, she hasn't changed. She told me her last two boyfriends, since me, were married guys with kids. One of whom she repeatedly slept with in the workplace! To the point people knew about it and would give her disgusted looks as she walked into work. Not surprised. I'm so embarrassed and ashamed to have ever been associated with such a scumbag. However, back to the point, she messaged me and wanted to meet up.

I 100% knew what the shctick was, but I wanted to see it for myself. Regarding the psychologically aspect, she is looking for 'supply', i.e. narcissistic supply, basically, attention. Once she gets her 'fix', like a vampire to blood, she will move on to the next victim. I knew this was what it was but I played along to see what would happen.

"Sure, I'll meet you. What did you want to do," I asked.

"Let's do something wild. Let's meet up and drive somewhere, maybe to a haunted mansion for a night, or camping in the woods," she suggested.

My thought was one of two things. A) she was painting a picture of a romantic spontaneous night with alcohol and passion. This was intended to lure me in and, really, paint the picture of an exciting evening. Or b) a plot to kill me.

Seriously, I thought the latter was an option out there. I played along, and the days went by as it drew closer, and she kept talking about it.

"We can sit on the roof of the car and smoke cigarettes and look at the stars," she'd suggest.

Very romantic. Very cool sounding. Though, I knew, it was just a game. She wanted my attention; she wanted my admiration;

she wanted me to fall for her again. But, I played along, knowing she would cancel on me the night before – 100%. I knew the game.

The night before came, and nothing; the day of the 'planned fake event' arrived, and nothing.

So I threw out a message, "Are we still on for later?" I knew the response was going to be, "Oh, it's my fault because I didn't plan it and I've made other plans."

Low and behold, her response was, "Oh, I didn't hear from you, so I've made plans to look after my sister's kids."

I chuckled to myself. I'd seen the game play out in real time. It was a week-long game to control one's emotions, to manipulate, and to get that much needed 'supply'.

Narcissists are incredibly weak, insecure, lonely, and bored individuals. They need these games to prop up their self-esteem. What's more worrying is that they are playing these games to multiple people, all at the same time. They are probably on their phones every other minute, messaging at rapid speed, playing the game with various people at once. They are homewreckers.

Impressed with my foresight, I played along and didn't react to it. Days later, she came back with a new proposal. "Let's go on holiday together." and "Let's meet after work to plan it." The latter was a plan to meet at 4 P.M., and she was messaging me until 3 P.M. about a location.

Later: 3:45 came, no answer; 4 P.M. came, no answer; 4:45 a message comes through, "I'm so sorry but I've had to stay late, let's rearrange." Games. Nothing but games. I had started driving home at 3:55 because I knew it was a game. A psychological game to control one's emotions, control one's time, and just generally get that 'one up' on the other person.

The point is, I understand the disorder of narcissism, and I can manage my own expectations of these scumbags. Their patterns are predictable. I imagine that if I didn't know about narcissism, these types of manipulation tactics would be incredibly hurtful. In fact, they're disappointing even when I know the let-down is going to happen! Even with that foresight, it is still hurtful. But if I didn't expect it, I can imagine it being much worse.

Don't expect anything from a narcissist. I have a video on YouTube called 'How to Disarm a Narcissist', and really the whole idea is to disarm them and take the play from them. Don't let them play these games with you. Don't ask anything of them; don't expect a compliment from them; don't joke around with them; don't communicate with them. Treat them like a robot. That's exactly what they are, a soulless robot.

Furthermore, if you're upset with a Narcissist, you can never shout at them or hurt them. They are indestructible. Why? Because they are already destroyed. They are nothing; they have nothing left. Nothing to savour or protect. If you show anger or sadness to a narcissist, they will laugh at you. They will happily absorb pleasure from your pain. As much as it would feel amazing to seek revenge and make them pay – it is to no avail. In fact, they will laugh at you from the grave when you are in jail. They want to ruin your life.

Educate yourself on the topic of narcissism. Understand narcissists, and you will obtain a power like no other. You will be able to predict their movements, their responses, their actions, and you won't feel hurt when they disappoint you. There's a lot of great content out there on YouTube, on Google, on Amazon. You can check out my eBook 'Behind the Mask: An Introduction into

Covert Narcissism' and there are hundreds of other books out there on the topic. Learn as much as you can.

My own personal journey was saved by the insight of covert narcissism. I spiralled into a depression due to an incredibly toxic individual in my life – this person was so bizarre and so passive aggressive, I didn't know what was going on. I spoke to people about it, but they didn't understand; they thought I was the crazy one for 'over thinking' things, but I knew something was up.

I then stumbled upon a video on covert narcissism on YouTube, and it sounds so cliché, but it changed my life. I was working on my novel at the time, but it took on a new life when I learnt about covert narcissism. I became obsessed with the topic. Everything was a lightbulb moment. I watched hours of content on YouTube, and the more I learnt I just couldn't believe how the traits were identical to the actions of this person who was the cause of so much weird psychological damage.

I realised then that there wasn't an awful lot of content available on 'covert narcissism,' so I made my own video discussing the traits. I just hope that anything I write will have the same light-bulb moment for other people who have suffered or are suffering from narcissistic abuse.

In terms of your contact with a Narcissist, you may have gone No Contact with them, but there will still be people in your life with narcissistic tendencies. Keep an eye out for warnings, and tread carefully around people who show certain character traits. Remember, if you have a suspicious feeling about someone, then you're probably right. Your gut instinct, your subconscious, is a very powerful tool. It's important you listen to it.

# CHAPTER 9
## STEP SEVEN – SET BOUNDARIES

Often, what happens in your childhood will stay with you for the rest of your life. Whether it's consciously or subconsciously, a lot of behaviours are established early on. Which makes sense; you're new to the world and learning, and whether you learn the good, bad, or the ugly, it may take you years to build up a frame of reference relating to your early experiences.

I recently did a YouTube video about a theory called, 'The Masochistic Equilibrium'. The idea behind this is you will purposely sabotage yourself in your adult years to align your level of comfort to that of which you experienced when you were a child.

For example, imagine you were raised in a very loud, hostile environment, with minimal physical contact and minimal praise. During those years, you would have found a level of comfort within that situation, not to mention a lack of reference to how 'normal' things should be. You learnt to survive in your childhood years under those conditions. You may even have been happy in those years. Often, people say things like, 'I didn't know anything different; this is normal to me' when asked how they coped with difficult circumstances.

"The Masochistic Equilibrium" is the theory that when you're older, you will purposely sabotage your life to get the same level of comfort, for better or worse, that you experienced as a child. Almost as if you are regressing to that childhood comfort state.

A lot of your memories as a child stick with you, for better or worse, and at times it can be the haunting memory of one particular incident that stabs your heart and brings back those haunting feelings of worthlessness. A good friend of mine has always struggled with his confidence. To this day, in his early 30s, he struggles with self-esteem. He is very cynical when starting new things, always sees the negative and, in short, doesn't believe in himself.

He speaks of his experiences with his father, how his father would bully him and undermine him. When my friend wanted to join the local football team to get fit, make new friends and have fun, his father would shoot him down, "No point in you doing that, you'll never get anywhere"; "You're not good enough to play football"; "You're too small to compete". Comments like these are extremely damaging. A child doesn't understand the concept of an abusive parent. It's almost as if there is belief the parent must unconditionally love their child, as if it is a divine right. This is not the case; and at times, parents hate and resent their children. A narcissistic parent will do anything to undermine their child; they wouldn't want their child to be more successful than they are; that would be a nightmare to the parent.

My friend said his father wouldn't take him to football, wouldn't take him to clubs, and never supported him on new endeavours. My friend pinpoints one particular scenario, which had a major impact on him. It sounds relatively minor, but it has clearly had a lasting impression on my friend, even 25 years later, when he tells the story he trembles and is close to tears.

He was once playing with his friends, having a good time, and it must have been fairly late, maybe 6-7 P.M., clearly past my friends curfew. he tells me his dad marched over a hill, saw them from afar, and screamed at him in front of his friends, "Get here now! What do you think you're doing?? Get over here right now!!"

It sounds minor, but that situation alone ruined my friend's confidence for the next 25 years, and is still an ongoing condition.

In the previous chapter, I discussed the importance of learning and studying narcissism. This will help you to identify narcissists and manage your expectations of them. Knowledge a very powerful thing. In the words of Sun Tzu, 'Know Your Enemy'.

Often, people won't have researched narcissism unless they have been severely scolded by one repeatedly over a period of time, to the point where they reach rock bottom and feel they need answers.

People learn behaviours as a child, and as an adult bring those feelings and behaviours with them. As you grow and your circumstances develop, you may have some context on where you want to be and how you want to behave. I believe role models and good friendship circles are important for this. That's one thing as a child you won't have had and you can implement that context as an adult when you're setting boundaries.

You need to set boundaries for yourself. Boundaries are your rule book. How far can someone go before you defend yourself? We are always taught to 'respect your elders', with which I agree, but not if those elders are bullying you. My mother, still to this day, doesn't understand why I'm No Contact with certain individuals. Her comment is, "They're older than you, so they can say and do anything they want to you." Seriously, that's what my mother says. Bless her soul. But sadly, that is a cultural mindset, a very old-fashioned mindset that doesn't fit in with modern day, and it shouldn't have fit in then. We need to promote a world of respect.

I had an abusive uncle who would verbally make fun of me and undermine me. Of course, he'd do so very passive aggressively and very 'I'm just joking, but deep down, I'm not joking', kind of way. I'm assuming because he was my uncle he knew I couldn't answer him back.

Not anymore. I had another family member who has been a lifelong bully – undermining, abusive, threatening, and utterly disrespectful. But, no more.

I didn't have boundaries as a teenager. I didn't know what they were. I thought my mother was right, perhaps this is just the order of life; but in adult life, you set those boundaries. If anyone is rude, passive aggressive, or offensive, I will look that person straight in the eye and say, 'NO'. Even if it's a subtle comment, I will call them on it, and I will do it publicly – which is exactly what the narcissist doesn't want. If someone crosses a line, betrays you, is openly offensive, then there's no need to play politics; you tell them EXACTLY how you feel.

I've made a clear point of setting boundaries for myself. And in truth, it feels good. I treat everyone with love, courtesy, and respect. But if that line gets crossed, I will defend myself. The reaction I've had since being this way has been a positive one. I feel like my friends value my opinions more, respect my space, and, in truth, it's a sign of integrity. Stand up for yourself; don't let anyone push you around.

Create those rules for yourself and stick to them. It's an empowering feeling. Often, we become the victim because we stay silent. We don't confront the passive aggressive scumbags; we don't talk to anyone about it due to fear of something. Don't worry about that. If someone does something wrong, stand up and look them straight in the eye. Or if it's digital, message them and ask them what issue they have with you. About 9 out of 10 times, they will deny it; they will apologise, and they will cower. RULE #1 of Narcissists: THEY ARE COWARDS. They really are.

Boundary setting puts you at risk of being accused of being 'hyper sensitive' and lacking a 'sense of humour', but it's important to know these comments will come from the abuser themselves. You are taking the game away from them and they're not going to like it. Narcissists, deep down inside are very weak individuals. They are imposters trying to appear as something with courage and integrity. There's a phrase, often used to describe narcissists (and toxic people), 'Wolves in Sheeps clothing'. In my opinion, narcissists are 'SHEEP in Woles clothing'. They are weak and frail, unlike a wolf. The wolf can stand alone if he needs to, the wolf has courage, the wolf is bold, the wolf has a clear set of rules he lives by. Narcissists are the opposite of this. They are a frail sheep like creature, desperate to ruin other peoples lives.

I'm going to touch on a darker topic, and I am keen to tread lightly on this topic out of respect to those who have suffered. There will be times when the abuse you incur is physical and sexual. Attackers may manipulate you, perhaps blackmail you to stay quiet. As I mentioned earlier, youngsters don't know how to set boundaries due to a lack of context, but as an adult, those boundaries should be formulated – and if you haven't set them, then start doing it. If you feel like you are being blackmailed, made to feel guilty, manipulated, or put in situations you have no control over, CALL FOR HELP. This is exactly the type of behaviour we need to encourage. Speak up; call for help. Speak to someone. No matter how paranoid, afraid, ashamed, or scared you are, you must speak to someone. There are several numbers out there, which I will include at the end of this book (in the appendix) that you can reach out to for help.

If something is happening in the workplace, speak to someone, vocalise it. Setting those boundaries will stop the attacker from doing it again. It will breed justice; it will breed freedom for you. If you don't confront the attacker yourself, go to someone for help.

Have a think about boundaries. How far will you let someone go with you? It's not easy if you're in love with a manipulative person; it's not easy. You may be afraid of losing them for whatever reason. But stand up for yourself. Do it with your head held high and always stay diplomatic. Narcissists will want to take the high moral ground with you, if you start cursing and shouting (as tempting as that is), they will see that as a sign of weakness (and use it against you). It will add ammunition to their smear campaign – they will often record you doing it and show people as 'proof' of your real self. They will respond to you calmly and 'maturely'. Remember, they are all about manipulating, lying, and getting the upper hand on you. Don't give them that privilege.

When confronting a narcissist:


- Stay calm
- Clearly state why you're not happy
- Inform them on how they should have behaved
- Tell them how disappointed you are in them and how they've really let you down.

Narcissists won't like you morally 'telling them off', but do it and do it while staring them in the eye. Let them know you are serious. If you are texting, be clear and to the point.

Boundaries. Whenever you're in the midst of a narcissist, no matter how passive aggressive their comment, set those boundaries and make it clear so the narcissist clearly understands your position. You will be surprised at their reaction.

# CHAPTER 10
## STEP EIGHT – ACCEPT THE SITUATION / BE HONEST WITH YOURSELF.

The recovery process will take a long time. It is not an easy journey, and you will have roadblocks stalling your progress. Personally, it took me two to three years to get back to some type of mental normality. Even though I still have vivid dreams of the individuals from my past who caused so much damage, I'm in a much better place.

People underestimate the power of mental abuse. Even if the perpetrator means to do it or not, that mental damage stays with you for a long time. It's probably why so many have body image issues or self-esteem issues; it could stem back to something traumatic they experienced many years earlier.

I used all the techniques in this book to help me recover and get back some sense of self-esteem, but one of the things I knew I had to do was be completely honest with myself.

I told myself I need to look in the mirror and know who I am. Like, really, who am I? What do I stand for? What do I represent? Do I like myself? Is the person I'm portraying to the outside world the real me?

These questions will become distorted over time. People will try to tell YOU who you are. If you break away from the status quo, they will accuse you of being 'big headed'. If you try to do something adventurous, they will call you 'deluded'. If you do something different to what they or their friends from the village are doing, they will laugh at you and make fun of you, all the while hoping you fail. And guess what? If you don't fail, they will stay quiet. If you slip up, they will joke about it.

You need to take ownership of who you are. What are your dreams? What would you like to achieve? You define yourself. Don't let your past or your environment determine who you are.

Once upon a time, my life was all figured out. I was going to marry my girlfriend from Las Vegas. I was going to move to the States, and I was going to make a new life over there; that was my plan. But, for whatever reason, it all fell apart, and I had to start again. I jumped into a 'rebound' relationship, and ended up head first into a hornet's nest; a psychotic sociopath girlfriend who was, what I can only explain as, soul destroying. Add to that narcissists in the workplace and the family, and I was surrounded. It was close to rock bottom for me.

One of the hardest things is accepting what's happened. Narcissists will gaslight you, and you won't know they've been doing it for, in some cases, years.

I had a narcissist in the family who did it to me for years without me realizing it. My ex didn't reveal who she really was until two years in. It's an extremely humiliating thing. Extremely humiliating to have your time wasted, to have been manipulated, cheated, deceived, and lied to. Your instinct is to be angry, violent and just do anything you can to get revenge, but it's best not to. That's what they want. They want you to be upset by it. They want you to have been affected by it. If any of those individuals were reading what I was writing now, they'd be laughing. They'd be smiling. It's a sense of victory for a narcissist to know they have affected someone's life.

But remember, the best way to beat those losers is do well, be a good person, try to be successful, have big dreams, and be happy. Narcissists won't be able to do any of those things – especially the "be happy" part. Your will and determination will cause resentment and hatred. Just go No Contact and let them watch on. (They are stalkers, so 9/10 they will be reading this).

You need to accept the situation. The past is in the past. You must let it go. Life doesn't always work out the way you want. In fact, I'm sure all of us are living a life that isn't what we planned. We hit crossroads; life throws curveballs at us; we have to adapt, things change, we grow, people grow, the environments change. Life is full of surprises, good and bad, but mostly good. I'd say if you wrote a list of the good and bad things in your life, you'd have more blessings in your life. The mere fact you are here on Earth is a victory in and of itself. Many millions of sperm don't make it to The Promised Land, but you're here. I'm here (for now) and well, this is a gift. Life outweighs any problem you can have.

Accept your situation. There is always someone out there who is going through worse. I know it may sound patronising, because our problems are important to us and affect us, but remember, you are not alone. Other people are suffering, too, in varying degrees. Accept that you encountered a scumbag narcissist and keep moving forward.

After my situation, I had nothing left. I had to rebuild. I had to soul search. What am I here to do? Where am I going? The irony is, if none of that had happened, I wouldn't be writing this today.

It started a journey of raising awareness for narcissistic abuse. This gives my life a purpose. It's extremely humbling that through what I went through, I can help others.

I had to be honest with myself. That also means I had to be honest with my mistakes. It's easy to distort the past to make yourself out to be the innocent one, but at times, we are not innocent. We make mistakes; we did things wrong; we did things we regret.

Even in an argument, perhaps we said something we regret, perhaps we shouldn't have had that argument. Perhaps we overreacted. I listed all my mistakes. I wrote them and read them. It was one of the hardest things I ever did.

I had a list of mistakes, and I realised the start of my downward spiral was partly my fault. Not entirely, but partly, and I admitted this to myself. I needed to admit that to be able to understand myself, to forgive myself, and to build my self-identity again.

By being honest with yourself, you can lay your cards out on the table and start again. As the phrase goes, 'it's not how many times you fall down, it's how many times you fall down and get back up'. This exercise also helps us to avoid creating a victim culture. It's important not to see ourselves as a 'victim'; this is, to me, a self-deprecating term that can cause resentment to those looking in. Instead, use the term 'target'. We were the target of someone else, specifically a psychologically damaged, person's self-destructive, jealous, insecure manipulative ways. THEY are the real victim. Why? Because they are deluded, shallow, bitter, insecure, soulless, disconnected, jealous, lonely, and depressed. They want others to feel the same way they do. THEY are the victims. They are losers who don't deserve credit for anything.

Anyone on the receiving end of a narcissist's ways is often an innocent, good-natured person, who, due to their good nature, doesn't see they are being gaslighted or manipulated. Or, they just don't like conflict and are trying rational methods to fix the situation. Methods that will never work with a narcissist because rational thinking doesn't work on them.

Narcissists wouldn't be able to write a list of their mistakes. They justify all their actions and feel they are 'perfect'. Literally, the notion of a narcissist making a mistake is unfathomable. I'd love to see that, actually. The list would probably be things like, 'I regret those things happened', 'I regret that person felt that way, but that's on them'. I'm not sure, I can only imagine they'd always put the blame and the onus on the other person. In their head, they are perfect. They are the Gods, the Kings and Queens of society.

Being honest with oneself is something narcissists can't do. So, you do it. Be the better person. Be the stronger person. It's a powerful action. List your mistakes and learn from them. Understand them. Highlight them. Don't run away from them. Don't be like a narcissist, who bury their head in the sand, ignoring other people's accomplishments, preying on people's weaknesses. Be a good person who encourages others, admits when you're wrong, learns, loves, laughs, and isn't afraid to make mistakes. Life is a journey. Don't get stuck in the mud simply to maintain some type of fake appearance. Life is too short for that. The whole point of recovery is to build a stronger version of yourself. You can only do that with clarity, knowledge, and 100% honesty.

# CHAPTER 11
## STEP NINE – CHANGE YOUR PARADIGM

Ever since I was a kid, I was fascinated by the concept of the paranormal. The question is still out there, and we probably all question it: Do ghosts exist? Everyone has their own story, an experience, a situation, an encounter, but we still don't have, and probably never will have concrete evidence.

These ghost hunting shows are funny because they are an hour long, and by the end of it, they see a small dot, or a white flash, and call it a ghost. For me, unless I see a fully formed Ghost standing there, talking to me like Casper, then I'm still on the fence.

However, that isn't to say there isn't power to spirituality. When I was going through my darkest hours, I sought great comfort from the idea of a 'God' and the idea that my life's problems were merely a test for greater and better things. There was great comfort in the idea that 'God's Time and Vision' was vaster than mine, and I should trust what is around the corner.

I went to church, and I listened to the services. Even though I'm not religious, I just wanted to experience something different and get a different perspective on things. At the very least, I wanted to be surrounded by positive and hopeful people. Actually, writing The Devil In I made me research the Bible and the story of God versus the Devil. That whole realm has been fascinating to me.

I see how religion is the cause of so much conflict in the world. People are so passionate about their beliefs and feel they have all the answers. I'm not here to speak about religion. But, the idea of a universal God, a master of the universe, to me, is comforting. I sometimes ask myself, if the universe started with the Big Bang (which is possible), what created the thing that went 'bang'? In the laws of physics and quantum physics as we know it, something can't just appear from nothing, can it? There would had to have been a creator?

Exploring spiritual things helped shift my paradigm, which is an important thing to do. I'll give you an example of how subtle a change of perspective can be on your life. Take for example, you are working in an office. You are sitting at the table, and next to you is your manager. You both are seeing almost the same thing; you are hearing the same thing; you are sitting in the same type of chair at the same desk. Your conditions, whilst one metre apart, are almost identical.

However, your experience is not the same. Your manager's perspective is completely different to yours (I assume). They have a completely different list of objectives and are viewing things in a different way.

Going along with that same theory, you may be at a concert with 15,000 other people – hearing, smelling, seeing the same thing. But the experience is going to be very different for each of you. There'll be several reasons for that. One person may have an obsession with the lead singer. Another person may be a tag along in a group and not too interested. Someone may be experiencing their first gig. One of those people may be the tour manager who's seen the show a thousand times. I hope I'm making sense: same situation, different paradigm.

Changing your outlook is an extremely powerful thing, and you can do that in so many ways. One of the ways I did it was trying to see life in a different way. I'd never been to church before, so I wanted to go and not only that, I went to several different ones. I'm not religious at all. I wouldn't call myself part of any type of religion, but the positive energy was good for me. I even spoke with Mormons (or Latter Day Saints) and got their book, 'The Book of Mormon'. I love Mormons because they are so friendly. Literally, they are the friendliest people out there, which is great when you've been surrounded by negative, dark, soul destroying scumbags for so long. It's refreshing to be around people who are happy and encouraging.

I embarked on a spiritual journey, and I'd encourage others to do so, too. I made great friends along the way. One of my best friends is a member of Iglesia Ni Christo, a Filipino based Christian church. Their service was extremely positive. We talk often and I always ask him a lot of questions about faith, we discuss all different things.

I met a man out in Los Angeles who is a member of the Seventh Day Adventist Church. To this day, we speak from time to time, and he's shared a lot of seminars and articles with me. To me, it's all good, and it's all interesting.

People say it's odd I have friends like this when I've written a book about the Devil. But my book is fiction and really, ultimately, the Devil doesn't win; in my book, the good guys prevail.

Being spiritual helped open my mind and see there is positivity out there. There are good people out there who want the best for you. It's good to have this outlook. I'm not saying become religious. I hope this isn't coming across like that, but reach out for new things.

I found travelling was a powerful way of growing the mind. Seeing different cultures, eating different foods, experiencing different environments are very soul enlightening experiences. Come to think of it, if I didn't take a risk and go to Las Vegas, eight days after having neck surgery – I wouldn't have met the girl I was going to marry. That wouldn't have developed into the train wreck my life became, and I probably wouldn't be writing this right now. So, my travelling at that time has had such an impact. It's like Chaos Theory. A ripple in the ocean can cause a storm further down the line. It's so true.

Think of things that have happened in your life, whereby, if they hadn't happened, you wouldn't be in the situation you're in now. Good and bad. It works both ways. Often, it's a situation from a situation that developed from something minor and coincidental.

What's to say something you do now won't have that same affect? That trip to the coast, where you go to a church, where you meet someone who becomes the love of your life, with whom you have a home (hypothetically). Anything can happen. Do something today. Plan something. You won't see its benefits now, but a few years down the line, something may have come from it which will make you think, 'Oh yeah'. And if that is the case, you'll remember this paragraph for the rest of your life.

Changing your paradigm will help give you a new perspective on life. Simply seeing something different or seeing someone else's views can help grow your own viewpoints. I guess that's the point of this chapter, to change your perspectives, be open to new things, and embark on a journey of discovery. I'm sure you'll get a lot out of that, as I have.

# CHAPTER 12
## STEP TEN – LET GO AND HAVE FUN!

When you've been trapped in the web of a toxic relationship for so long, you will almost forget there's a world out there. A world with so much opportunity and things to explore. We become so absorbed in our own lives, and in fact, the world of others, we forget there is a possibility to drop it all and start again.

There's a story I once heard that brings a smile to my face. It was of a man who had lost everything. He got divorced; he got disconnected from his kids; he filed for bankruptcy. He was abandoned by his family. He lost his job. He had nothing left. He had decided he wanted to kill himself. He had nothing else to live for and couldn't see a way out. However, before he kills himself, he decides he's going to draw out the remains of his life savings and travel to Mexico. He then planned to spend all of his money on partying, and then afterwards kill himself.

So, he did just that. He flew to Mexico, partied hard, met loads of new people, had fun and blew every penny. What happened to the guy was, he was no longer suicidal! He enjoyed this life so much, he decided to stay and, to my knowledge, he's still alive now. It's a slightly crude message, and I don't advocate that type of plan, but it's a nice reminder that 'there's always a way out'. You may have hit the end of the road, but that doesn't mean there's not another road that can't be embarked on.

We change all the time, every two years, probably. Our circumstances, our life, our experiences (the good and the bad) mold us into something we previously couldn't have imagined. There are countless stories of people whose lives drastically changed overnight. You need to believe this will be the case for you. You won't always see that. It's hard to envisage your life changing sometimes, and those frustrations can lead to depression and anxiety. But, if your heart is open and your mind is ready to absorb new things – things will absolutely change. You simply must trust the process.

Letting go of the past is one of the hardest things you can do. You may still be in love with the narcissist; you may want revenge on them; you may be feeling guilty for going 'No Contact'; you may be working in the same environment they are; you may even be going through a divorce and have children together. Letting go is never easy; and nobody said it's supposed to be.

However, there are steps to take that can help you let go and move on with your life. If you're still in love with them, you need to ask yourself why you would feel attached to someone who caused you so much pain and mental distress. You know that narcissists gaslight; you know they mirror you; you know they manipulate you. There's no way out. I know many people who are still in love with the narcissist who was once in their life, and I appreciate that once those wires of love are sown, they are hard to undo. It can take years to unravel, but you need to keep reminding yourself what has happened. You have fallen in love with an illusion.

If you are going through a divorce and have children with a narcissist, this will require you to be strong and set boundaries.

Any abuse or offensive messages you hear need to be flagged to the police. Any violation of terms and conditions need to be flagged. Almost take a robotic approach to it. Keep a journal of all negative actions, noting the date and time. This will help should you need to go to court. The narcissist will try to manipulate you, make you feel guilty, make you second guess your actions – and all the while being aggressive with you and inconsistent. Don't let them ruin your happiness. No one has a right to disrupt your happiness. Anything you're going through, play it by the book. Follow the rules and trust that the law is there to protect you. It won't be easy; whenever children are involved, it can get very ugly, very quickly. Also, be sure not to disparage your ex in front of the children. This can be used against you, but most importantly, the children don't need to be in the fight.

If you work with a narcissist who is damaging you or have narcissist parents or family member, you need to go No Contact. The hard part about this is, especially in the work place, you'll have to leave friends behind. There's no other way; the narcissist is often too influential in workplace environments due to their manipulative skills. You won't be able to compete with them. If you do, it will result in fireworks and total psychological warfare.

The sad truth is, you have to walk away. It will feel like a defeat at first, but you will grow and prosper into something much better. You can't excel in the workplace when there are toxic narcissistic people in the immediate vicinity. They will ensure you are kept down and pigeonholed – and more importantly for them, ensure you do not exceed them.

With family members, it is even harder to go No Contact, but not impossible. You can still maintain a healthy relationship with the rest of your family, but be warned, if the narcissist is manipulating them against you, you may lose those family members, too. You need to make tough decisions, but ask yourself, what's more important than your sanity? Why be in any relationship, in any form, if it is causing you to go insane? It's simply not worth it. Nothing is worth your sanity. Life is a gift; the people with whom you choose to share it, should love and respect who you are, and in turn, you treat them with harmony and love. You can enjoy great times and build memories with the ones you love. Anyone who doesn't fit into that category should not be given any level of thought or attention.

It sounds cliché, but you must go out there and have fun. Don't self-destruct; simply have fun. Go into your car and drive somewhere far. Meet new people, have some drinks, have fun. So much of our life is controlled by people who think they know what is best for you. We are controlled by fear, fear of the unknown, fear of losing everything, fear of bankruptcy, fear of dying. People live in fear.

Just look at home insurance. We pay a monthly premium for…nothing. For the fear of what could happen. Have you ever used it? Probably not. It's important to let go of the shackles of fear and live your life. Write a list of the things you've always wanted to experience and go out and do them. The happiness and wisdom those things will give you will give you strength. It will ensure the 2.0 version of yourself is stronger and happier. In the decisions you made, it starts with you.

# BEHIND THE MASK: AN INTRODUCTION INTO COVERT NARCISSISM

*Dedicated to anyone who has betrayed my trust.*
*You are a constant source of motivation.*

# INTRODUCTION

Hello and thank you for purchasing "Behind the Mask: An Introduction into Covert Narcissism." If you have got this far, you have probably encountered the wrath of a covert narcissist. I started doing YouTube videos to help spread the word about narcissistic abuse and how damaging it can be. I still don't believe the mainstream media quite understand what a covert narcissist is and how evil and damaging these people can be.

If you have been unlucky enough to have suffered from narcissistic abuse, then I know your pain. The feelings of hopelessness, low self-esteem, and constant search for answers is something with which only those who've experienced it can empathize. The feelings of having someone plot against you and you being powerless to change it are traumatic. If you are anything like me, at one point in your life you have felt lost and on the edge.

I decided to put this e-Book together to compile all of the content from my YouTube videos into one readable package. This will allow you to refer back to the content, which will help you with your research into covert narcissists.

My number one goal with this is to **spread the word**. Please, share this e-book, get it out there, show your friends, and talk about it with family. The only way we can make this topic known to the mainstream is to keep talking to people about it. The mainstream need to know.

My passion to help people who have suffered narcissistic abuse started five years ago when I started writing my book "The

Devil in I." The book isn't about narcissism, but its main characters are narcissists. The book is about a character called Damon West who is the Devil. He lives a normal life: he has a job, a girlfriend, and friends - but he is in fact the Devil. Damon's life quickly starts to fall apart when he falls for a girl in his workplace. He doesn't understand these new emotions and finds himself ill-equipped to deal with them. Damon's sensational life starts to spiral out of control, and the story follows this demise. He loses his job, his girlfriend, and his freedom.

The book started off as a thesis on Good and Evil; it didn't really have an 'unrequited love' arch to it, until I myself encountered an extremely complex individual who left me completely confused and damaged. It took a long time to get over it and understand what was going on. Feelings of hate, resentment and depression consumed me. What appeared insignificant and nothing to others took over my whole life. So, I decided to write that in to the story.

This individual stalked me relentlessly, would flirt with me and message me non-stop at all hours, yet all the while was talking negatively about me to others. This was damaging my reputation. It was an extremely complex and 'screwed up' situation. I didn't understand what was happening nor why it was happening. It was as if I was being bullied, but I didn't quite know if I was. Anytime I retaliated verbally or asked what was going on, I was accused of being 'crazy' and 'paranoid' (we will go into what this means later).

This opened up the doors for research. I started looking at anything I could find, and I stumbled upon a video on something called 'Covert Narcissism'. I guess my life changed from that point. I was obsessed with this topic; I read every article, watched every YouTube video and absorbed every bit of content I could find about covert narcissism. EVERYTHING in these videos linked into this person - it was incredible. I felt a sense of justice. I started mentioning this topic to some friends, and to my surprise - no one knew what it was. No one.

The crazy thing is, the more I learnt about Covert Narcissism the more I realized another person in my life was one of these evils. This particular person is someone I've known for years and has always been a source of constant mental struggle for me, just an evil bully who thrives on making others feel bad. I've seen this bully swear and shout at old ladies in public. I've seen this person call a mother with kids 'a slut and a whore' in front of her own kids. I've seen this woman beat her own kids. I've seen this woman bully others, say the most awful things, and then cry uncontrollably afterward as if 'SHE' is the victim. It makes my blood boil that after all these years, I couldn't see it. This person sent me to the edge. A place where I could not defend myself, a place where I felt lost and imprisoned. A place where any self-confidence or pride in myself was trampled on. A place which left me contemplating my own life. I'm sure you have felt the same in your experiences.

The mainstream seem to think narcissism is when someone loves themselves, which is inherently true. But narcissistic abuse and malignant narcissism is so damaging, so evil, it can actually leave lives in tatters.

Since doing YouTube videos, it's been very humbling to see the comments about people's personal experiences and how they have been able to relate to the content. It's great to see and we are bound by the same passion - to find answers! Why do these people carry out such horrible acts? What are they? Why do they abuse people? How can we stop them?

So here we are, doing everything we can to expose the behaviours of covert narcissists. I am not a professor in psychology, and I don't claim to be. I don't have all the answers - but I am someone who has experienced this first hand by two separate people. Years of analysis and passion to expose these people has led me to this point. I can empathize with victims of narcissistic abuse because I have been there and am still suffering the remnant. Like you, all I want is answers and closure.

I have split the e-Book into chapters that will discuss the overriding themes of covert narcissism. I thank you from the bottom of my heart for purchasing this e-Book. Let's work together to expose covert narcissists. Spread the word, share it, email it out, and get everyone talking about it. We can do this. I sincerely hope the content of this book helps you find peace and freedom in your life.

# CHAPTER 1
# HOW TO SPOT A COVERT
# NARCISSIST

Identifying a covert narcissist is extremely difficult. Everything they do is disguised. It may take you years to know if you are in the presence of a covert narcissist. Furthermore, humans are not easy to 'pigeon hole'. There are psychopaths (people with borderline personality disorder), people with Asperger's syndrome, overt narcissists, sociopaths and people with subtle tendencies in some of these things.

The spectrum is so wide, it's hard to say, 'Yes, this person is a narcissist, they tick all of these boxes'. It's more complex than that. You may have someone with narcissistic tendencies who may be relatively healthy. Or someone may be a covert narcissistic but also a violent psychopath. It really depends. Having narcissistic tendencies is very different to having NPD (Narcissistic Personality Disorder). There is no one way of pigeon holing people. Everyone is different, and the level of psychological damage within the person can vary. Some people may have elements of each psychological disorder or have characteristics that interlink. Humans are extremely diverse and complex individuals, and it's important to be aware of that. The scholars I've spoken to on this subject are, at times, defensive on psychology topics. They say things like, 'Covert narcissists are ALWAYS like this', "Overts

ALWAYS do this', 'Coverts ARE ALWAYS this' etc. I'm paraphrasing, of course, but I feel the scholars need to have an open mind. Humans are very complex forces - with varying degrees of behaviour and background. You can't pigeon hole anyone or anything, especially when it comes to psychology. Psychology is a constantly moving force with wide spectrums.

Not every covert narcissist is malignant all of the time but they are all capable of inflicting serious psychological damage. You will hear me refer to 'narcissistic rage' in this eBook; this is the dark side of a narcissist. Some people are just incredibly negative, depressive, and nihilistic - not necessarily a 'covert narcissist', but it's important to know the traits of a covert narcissist and to apply it where you see fit.

In this eBook, I offer my opinions, which are based on years of research (from multiple sources), hours of videos and articles, and firsthand experience from malignant covert narcissists.

If there is anything in this book that helps you in your research, then this has achieved its goal.

Let's look at some key characteristic of the covert narcissist.

## They Look Perfect

The interesting thing about covert narcissists is that they appear to have no insecurities. In essence, they are revealing to the world, and themselves, that they are the 'Perfect Being'. If only it could be so simple, right? Well, it's not! They may appear perfect and fully content with their lives, but they are not. In fact, they are quite the opposite.

They HATE themselves. A covert narcissist is riddled with insecurity and a constant need for acceptance. They desire narcissistic supply, a constant supply of compliments and praise. To get this, they will do anything. They will look great, they will work out, they will say all the right things and they will appear 'perfect'.

On the surface, they may very well be perfect. A mother, a home, a successful husband, a business of their own, a great personality - a 'success story'. But there is more to it below the surface.

They despise who they are. They are wearing the narcissistic mask. As soon as that mask slips, you will see their true colours. Many have mentioned the narcissistic stare; an evil cold stare that is seen once in a blue moon.

What is going on beneath the surface with these coverts? This is not as simple as them 'hating themselves' - there is a paradigm and an internal. On the one hand, they are completely unfulfilled. They haven't achieved what they've wanted in life. They are stuck in a town, with no ambitions, no hope, nowhere to go. Things around them have fallen apart; life didn't pan out to their grand expectations. Somewhere along the way, they have picked up an insecurity. Whether it's abuse from an early age, whether it's the way their life has panned out, or whether they were simply born this way - they have a burning insecurity inside them. But. want me to confuse you more? They have a feeling

of self-entitlement! Their social interactions hide all of these insecure feelings. They actually believe they are better than everyone else.

A narcissist doesn't show their insecurity, not in an obvious way. Oddly enough they do have a self-deprecating sense of humour. They will openly say things like 'I will die alone', 'No one wants me', and 'I suck at that', etc. But it's all just part of the Master Plan. They are allowed to self-deprecate because oddly enough, it's a social sign of confidence and light heartedness. The narcissist is appearing to not take themselves too seriously.

Where this shifts is; if anyone else says anything even remotely derogatory about these people, it will be met with rage and sadness. They will not be able to handle it and, in fact, will retaliate in a hostile manner.

They give advice to people as if their word is the Gospel. They have a God complex - *everything they say* is the Law of the Land. No one is more 'intelligent', 'experienced', as 'knowledgeable' or 'talented' as these individuals.

They will do anything to give this perception of 'success'. They will marry a Saint. What I mean by that is, they will marry someone who is successful and down to earth. They will gloat to others about this person, about how successful and 'high up' this person is; money and status is so important to the covert narcissist.

Covert narcissists are often promiscuous. This has two strands of psychology to it. First, they have a constant need to be wanted. It's the narcissistic supply. Being worshiped to a narcissist is like heroin to a heroin addict. They need it, they crave it, and their lives are fulfilled once they have it.

Secondly, it's a sense of control and power. Narcissists are complete control freaks. They need to control the elements around them, again, this fills them with joy and comfort. If they can control everyone around them, even their emotions, then they will feel like the Queen (or King). What better way to control someone than through love and sex?

Narcissists love control. So much so, they will manipulate the people around them and turn people against each other. This is often refered to as triangulation. I've seen narcissists literally burn a place to the ground (metaphorically) and come out looking like the victim. How do they do this?

They maintain a close-knit group of people around them who worship them (perfect for a narcissist). They are often refered to as 'Flying Monkies'. These people will believe EVERYTHING the narcissist says. It's the perfect defense mechanism. It allows them to not only control their 'friends', but it allows them to character assassinate everyone they wish to destroy.

It's important to be wary of the people around the Narcissist. People in their group can be just as dangerous as the narcissist themselves. All of the stalking a covert narcissist is known for, all of the behaviours they ilicit is portrayed by the loyal group of obsessed groupies around them. They will do the narcissists 'dirty work' – they will stalk you, talk bad about you and do everything to destroy your reputation. It's like a cult.

Covert narcissists only allow people into their lifes who they can control. These people are generally weak, sub-servient weaklings. Narcissists can't handle strong minded, opiniated people, they can't control those people. What tends to happen to people in the narcissists close circle is, they will be abused so bad, and become so obsessed, they will actually start to mimic their abuser. Not just that, but they will carry out the narcissists path of evil destruction. Covert narcissists are extremely manipulative.

Narcissistic siblings are very good at this. If it's a big family they will purposely say the most awful things about someone to family members and, of course, those siblings will believe it. It's very difficult to defend against it.

So, covert narcissists appear to be 'Perfect'. They look great, they talk great and they try to attach themselves to successful people. .It's important to note, it's rare that the covert narcissist is actually successful themselves. They just associate with successful people. It's normal for a covert narcissistic woman to marry a rich man or a man with status. They will attach themselves to this and feed off it. Remember, money and status is everything to a covert narcissist.

One thing I will leave this topic on is this. If something looks too good to be true, it is! Everyone has insecurities, everyone has flaws, and no one is perfect. If someone looks too good to be true, believe me, he/she is!

As in most things in life, remember: If it looks too good to be true, it really is.

## They are incredibly Jealous!

Covert Narcissists are incredibly jealous people. They cannot bare or even entertain the idea that anyone is more successful than they are. This is a constant struggle for the narcissist. Obviously, there is always someone more successful and better looking with more money in the world. Even billionaires are competing with each other.

Jealousy is an incurable trait of the narcissist. As previously discussed, money and status are incredibly important to them. They are also complete control freaks. So, what do they do? They will try to control the controllable.

Everyone around them will see them as Gods and Goddesses. If it's in the workplace, they will appear to be the 'fairest of them all'. Let's analyze the female narcissist. Now, if anyone in the workplace challenges the covert for beauty and reputation, a 'war' will break out. The one covert will take all of their cronies and character assassinate the other. The other covert will do exactly the same. So, what do we have? A workplace war.

Narcissists are incredibly jealous people. They need to appear to be the best at everything they do. If it's something they can't compete with, they will simply remove themselves from the situation. In the other instance, if it is something in which they can compete, they will talk about it to the Nth degree, berating on 'how' and 'what' to do and snigger if you don't have the same level of knowledge as they do.

Narcissists can't stand others to be happy. They will do everything to ruin happy relationships. A female narcissist will use her sexuality as a weapon to destroy stable homes.

Narcissists in general just consume life. They are complete parasites. If it's a particular music group they like, they will listen to it nonstop - they will ruin the hell out of that band until they're sick of it and then move on to the next.

Granted, I'm pretty sure most of us have done that, and it's probably not the best example to use but it's simply different with narcissists. They consume things and suck the life out of things. If they find a new passion in life, they will obsess over it and become an 'expert', talking about it to everyone nonstop, until it dries up. Then they move on to the next item. Like a sponge full of water, they will squeeze and squeeze until nothing is left in it. They are takers; they consume life in every way.

They enjoy doing it to humans, as well. They consume humans (not literally); they will suck them dry (again, not literally... well, maybe!) and leave the person with nothing left - no self-esteem, no money, no friends, nothing.

So, what do covert narcissists do to destroy people's lives?

If they feel like there is someone out there who is well respected and potentially 'better' than they are - they will seek to destroy. Again, they are JEALOUS.

They will do everything and anything to push people down. Firstly (and in no particular order), they will character assassinate you.

They will do this by saying awful things about you to their 'cronies' or 'henchmen' (or flying monkies). The covert narcissist can't bear the idea of anyone being better, so they will character assassinate that person. They will say awful things, play the victim, spread rumours and, at the end of it, they themselves will appear sweet as roses.

What the covert narcissist will do is actually do this publically; they will publicly shame and bully the person. They will do this covertly, in a way which appears as 'banter' or 'needling'. This makes it very difficult to defend against; if you take their comments seriously, you will be seen as being affected by the narcissists words, which further exposes your insecurities. The narcissist will relish in this, and once they know they can get to you, they will keep doing it.

Covert Narcissists are incredibly cunning (though, not nearly as much as they think they are). If they find out the one thing that is bugging you, the one thing that really cuts deep and hurts your feelings, they will find it. And they will keep pushing and pushing and pushing and pushing...until you're ready to explode.

If you react to it, the narcissist will LOVE IT. You are nothing more than a lab rat to the narcissist. They are great at finding what hurts you, and they will cut deep. They want you dead. They don't want you around them. If it appears you are better than them, they will do everything to get you removed! They don't like the idea of someone who appears superior to them being around. They are jealous to the core and will do everything to destroy the spark and confidence you have.

If you confront a narcissist for the things they say, they will simply deny it! "I was just joking,", "We're friends, I was only needling!" or "We're family, of course I only want good things for you!" It's all BS. They know exactly what they are doing. They are meticulously destroying your self-esteem. They don't want anyone to have confidence or self-esteem, because they themselves don't have any.

Secondly (again, not in any particular order), the covert narcissist will do anything to bankrupt you. They are the ultimate Gold Diggers. They will attach themselves to a wealthy man with status, only to destroy him. They'd even go as far as to have a child with this person so they can get child support from them. Remember the previous rule – they consume everything! If they can suck the life, blood, and money from someone, they will!

They will also live vicariously through these people. Other people's successes become their own. They themselves may not have achieved anything, but by proxy, they will absorb the other person's success.

The narcissist will often befriend popular people, wealthy people, and people with authority and status.

If you feel the wrath of a narcissist's jealousy, be prepared for everything and anything. They will go to great lengths to character assassinate you and to bankrupt you. They will do everything to leave you with no friends (as a result of the character assassination) and no self-esteem. Picking up the pieces from narcissistic abuse takes years and is very difficult to do.

Exposing covert narcissists is an important first step to recovery.

**They always want to be the centre of Attention!**

Covert Narcissists love attention. They need it, they crave it. This is their narcissistic supply. However, there is a tricky paradigm within the soul of a covert narcissist. They WANT and NEED to be the centre of attention, but they don't want to put themselves in a position of being JUDGED.

This leads to more covert behaviour. They can't overtly be the centre of attention because if they leave themselves open to scrutiny, the possibility of having others judge them is too hard to bare. So, what do they do? Well, they become the centre of attention, covertly.

They manipulate people around them, so much so that this person is talked about and discussed by these people. When the Covert Narcissist isn't there, they are being spoken about. This is a perfect situation for a Covert Narcissist. They need to be the centre of attention, even when they are not in the room!

They will Stir the Waters but remain untouched. They will create chaos around them, people will hate each other, people will fight with one another and resentment and rage will build up. But all the while, the covert narcissist is left untouched and looking 'perfect'. It is the ultimate God complex, they are effectively 'playing God'.

Remember the previous rules, they are jealous of anyone being better than them, and that includes being more popular. They need to be the most popular. They are ultimate control freaks - they are always trying to control everything around them. If they can't control something, they will literally spiral out of control. I've seen a covert narcissist literally pull their hair out and openly weep, like they are in a Shakespeare play. Life is just a performance to them.

Covert Narcissists are the centre of attention even when they are lurking in the shadows. They are the ultimate snakes in the grass. They enjoy using 'knowledge' and gossip as a way to manipulate people. They *always* know more about someone than other people - they have a great way of finding things out! Why? Because they stalk people. They will spend hours scouring the Internet and searching for anything they can find on this person that will be detrimental to their victim's reputation. And they will share it.

Narcissists hide in shadows but make no mistake, they are monitoring you. If they see you as a threat, they will monitor you and keep track of everything you are doing, everything, all whilst hiding in the shadows.

Covert Narcissists, like the Queen, King or God they see themselves, must always be on the edge of everyone's lips. This is when they know they have got you under their spell, which is a perfect and humbling achievement for the Covert Narcissist.

**They always play the victim**

One of the interesting things about Covert Narcissists, and this is a credit to their cunningness, is how they always come off as being 'the victim'. They act like the innocent, vulnerable sheep but inside they are a vicious wolf. The crazy thing is, they actually believe it. In their eyes, the whole world is against them. A covert narcissist will appear fragile and weak and openly discuss their sob stories to everyone.

"My partner doesn't love me", "My partner doesn't talk to me", "My partner never treats me to things", "my partner never shows me affection", "my partner doesn't understand me", "I have too much on in my life", "I have no time for myself", this plays into the smaear campaigns that coverts front.

They play the victim, and they'll often do this in a self-deprecating way: "I'm single and can't find a man", "I can't cope with my children!", "My life's too hard", "I have so much on"...it's all negative, constant sob stories. When in truth, their lives are perfectly normal compared to everyone else.

This topic extends to a more unfortunate situation (which will be discussed further on in this ebook). It's their ability to inflict serious harm on you, either mentally or physically, and then cower in fear when you respond. For example, a covert malignant narc will humiliate you - publicly or when you are alone with the person and whatever response you give, they will respond as if THEY are the ones being attacked. They will literally beat you down, but if you even raise a finger, they will quiver and shake in fear - playing the role of a vulnerable, innocent lamb when in fact they are anything but. The phrase, 'a wolf in sheep's clothing,' can't be truer when talking about a Covert Narcissist.

One of the things to always consider if you feel you may be in the presence of a covert narcissist, is that, what you are hearing from the Narcissist is one side of the story, their side. To heighten the bias, you're hearing a side from the covert narcissist who is oblivious and in denial of any wrongdoing. No matter what situation it is, THEY cannot do any wrong; they will never hold their hands up and admit they made a mistake. They cannot apologise, they have an inability to say sorry. If they do utter the words 'sorry', it will be insincere. They will phrase it like, "I'm sorry you feel that way", or, "I'm sorry you don't like my thoughts". They will never be held accountable for any slip ups; they will never say they are sorry! Furthermore, they won't accept apologies. Instead, they will emotionally abuse you and make you suffer for any mistake you may have made.

Covert Narcissists are wearing a mask. The mask is of a 'perfect being'. They will insult you, bully you, mentally damage you but any response will be seen as an attack on them. To further this, as I mentioned earlier, the narcissists hide behind people - their husbands, their bosses, their parents. It's impossible to stand up for yourself. If you were in a position to retaliate verbally, the covert will cower as if he/she is the victim. They're extremely manipulative, so they will cry, they will accuse you of the worst things. They will character assassinate you to their 'cronies' - they will make sure your reputation is destroyed.

They will also accuse you of the worst things. If you stand up to a covert narcissist verbally, they will accuse you of being 'a woman beater'. "He tried to beat me up!", "Call the cops!", "He wants to kill me!", "My life is in danger". These cowards will say anything as a defense mechanism. In reality, all you have done is verbally stand your ground but they will see this as an opportunity to 'play the victim' and ensure that in the process, not only will you be branded the aggressor, but your reputation and character will be tarnished.

Going back to what I was saying about hearing only one side of the Narcissist's story, I will give you a few examples of this.

I know a covert narcissist who has had several failed relationships - multiple. And in each one, it has ended so badly the men in question were driven to near insanity. One man became suicidal; the other was in constant tears. Every time I saw him, he was depressed and red eyed (from crying). The Covert, all the while, was happy and 'perfect'. When observing in hindsight, it was the Covert who drove these people to the edge and when they retaliated, in whatever form, the covert was the 'innocent victim'. If it happens once, then okay, but multiple times across several years shows a pattern. The men in question had their characters tarnished and assassinated; they were branded as the evil ones, the wrong ones - but looking back, it was a very different story.

Another example is of a covert who split with her partner. Every day this person's character was publicly assassinated, 'He does this,' 'He does that', "He's an alcoholic", 'He has no personality', to paraphrase. It led to everyone having a negative opinion about this person. And that's what covert narcissists do. They manipulate the people around them to influence things in their favour. They always appear to be the perfect ones, the untouched.

**They lack empathy**
Covert Narcissists lack empathy - but it's slightly more complex. Unlike a psychopath, they are still capable of feeling 'something' toward certain people; their kids, pets and their spouse. These feelings come from a selfish place. If the person in question gives them narcissistic supply, they will feel an attachment to this person or animal.

Pets. Covert Narcissists love pets, like dogs or cats. Why? Because the pet worships them. The dog, for example, sees the covert narcissist as their God. This is perfect for the Covert Narcissist. This is exactly the type of narcissistic supply the covert narcissist is looking for. In response to the dog's behaviour, the narcissist will ensure the dog is happy in order to keep receiving this praise.

It's the same with kids. Kids worship their parents. Kids are 100% dependent on the covert narcissist. The kids see their parents as the Gods of their world. Covert Narcissists love this. Are you noticing a trend? As long as the individual in question worships the Covert, the covert will react positively to that person or animal.

So, whether the Covert Narcissist has empathy or not doesn't really matter in these situations, they probably have a skewed, distorted version of 'empathy' when dealing with their children and pets. It would appear they do feel for these people and/or animals but make no mistake, it is for selfish means only.

The Covert Narcissist is very clever. They are bordering genius with their social performance. The narcissist is fully aware that 'showing a reaction' to something that would merit a reaction will highlight them in a positive light. They WANT to be seen as 'Loving', 'Caring' and the highest on the moral compass. So much so, that when they see something 'bad', they will react to it and they will visually present themselves as showing emotion and being distraught or upset. Whether they really mean it is unclear, they may have convinced themselves that they really do care. You know that 'stab to the heart' feeling you get when you feel empathy? In my opinion, covert narcissists don't feel that. I truly believe that.

Where it becomes more apparent that the covert narcissist lacks empathy is when they are confronted with someone or something they cannot control. If they can't control you, or if they can't manipulate the way you think then you will be as regarded as last week's trash. They have an ability to inflict the worst harm, the worst comments and the most vicious of taunts without feeling a thing for the other person's emotions.

I've seen a particular covert narcissist openly attack an old lady verbally. And when the old lady apologized, she refused her apology and slammed the door on her face. Hearing this story gives me that horrible shudder that a normal sane person would feel, but this cruel act happened. How shameful, vile, and disgusting. These people are monsters.

**Other signs to look out for**

There are several other things you can do to figure out whether you are in the presence of a covert narcissist.

**The Feeling Question**

One thing they will never do is ask, 'How are you feeling?' They aren't able to ask a question like this because their minds are not wired to care for others on an emotional level. They may ask you this question, but they won't mean it. They are probably doing it to gather information on you.

One thing about a Covert Narcissist, they are the best detectives. They will find any information on you! Furthermore, anything you say to a narcissist will be remembered and used against you in the future (if they can). They are incredible detectives with incredible memories. You are nothing more than a lab rat to the covert narcissist, and in a covert way, they will do anything and everything to completely destroy your self-esteem. If they can, they will do everything and anything to destroy your life and reputation.

**Intimacy**

When looking for a covert narcissist, which is an incredibly difficult thing to do, you can look for signs of intimacy. Covert narcissism is in some ways linked to psychopaths (borderline personality disorder), Asperger's, and sociopathic behaviors. A lot of these conditions intertwine.

When looking for a covert narcissist, perhaps you can look to see if you can imagine them being intimate with someone. This won't work with siblings (unless you're in Game of Thrones), but for anyone in the workplace or outside of the home, if you suspect they may have covert narcissistic traits, try to imagine kissing them.

This sounds a bit crazy - but give it a try. The reason behind this is, the narcs I've encountered aesthetically look good, but have no personality or soul. You can only kiss someone with soul (in my opinion). If someone has no soul, they are an empty vase and you won't be able to even imagine hooking up with that person.

## They will never admit fault

Covert Narcissists have trouble accepting any fault. In fact, they will *never* accept fault. They are incapable of apologizing. Their apologies are blaze and shallow - they won't mean any apology. They may say 'sorry' just to solve a problem or to sweep something under the carpet, but they won't actually mean it. They justify all of their actions.

Covert narcissists are always blaming others. If their life didn't pan out the way they had hoped - they will blame others. I know a covert narcissist who has a burning insecurity because her life never panned out the way she had hoped. She blames her family; she blames others for this. She has a grudge against them. She never once accepts that she didn't chase her goals - she just points the fingers at others.

Narcissists never accept fault. They believe they are the 'perfect being'. They believe any shortfalls or mistakes are the errors of others. If something doesn't work out the way they want, they believe it is someone else's fault. They always blame others.

## Chaos is always around them

Chaos is always around the covert narcissist. They are complete cowards so they will never confront anyone face to face on an issue - if they did, they will do it publicly with people around them - with their 'cronies' around them. Remember, Narcs love to hide behind others!

One particular Covert I am aware of always has issues around them. They are constantly falling out with people - they always launch smear campaigns against others. They go as far as showing private text messages to everyone around them to further character assassinate that person.

You will never meet a Covert Narcissist without enemies. They have a lot of enemies.

Chaos surrounds them; they are like the centre of the universe (their universe) and around them is storm and chaos. Everyone's life is ruined and impacted by the narcissist - but they are left untouched and 'perfect'. They are the ultimate stirrers; give them a metaphoric spoon and they will stir trouble wherever they go. It gives them a sense of power and achievement by having influence on someone else's life, even if that influence is negative.

## They don't think they can improve

Covert Narcissists don't think they can improve. One of the questions you can ask them is, "If you can improve three things about you, what would you improve?"

I asked this question to someone, and their response was extremely defensive and violent - the mask slipped and showed what was behind it.

"Who the hell do you think you are asking me that?" she said.

"I've never been patronized so much in my life!" she added. Her face scrunched and she was extremely offended.

Now, if you asked a non-Covert Narcissist this, they will list multiple things. I myself can list at least 20 things I can improve. I need to hit the gym more; I need to focus more; I need better attention skills; I want to work on more educational courses; I want to plan things better; I want learn more, etc. There are multiple things. It's actually a good question to ask yourself because you can identify areas that you can focus on to further enrich your life.

Ask a Covert Narcissist this and you will be in trouble! They don't believe they can improve. They truly believe they are perfect.

# CHAPTER 2
## CONTROL, TRIANGULATION, LIES AND SEX

**Control**

The covert narcissist loves to control you. They are the master manipulators of the world. They will say things, subtly, to hurt feelings. Any response from you would be seen as being 'overly sensitive', 'high strung' or 'too serious'. However, whatever they say to hurt your feelings is intentional.

A covert narcissist won't physically abuse you, that's a trait associated more with an overt. The damage a covert is interested in is psychological. They will make you feel bad. They will play the victim, they will act like an innocent sensitive sheep (how could anyone possibly hurt them!). While they act like this - they will emotionally control you, they will make **you** feel like the bully, they will make **you** feel like you're being aggressive. But all the while, there is a wolf in there, grinning from ear to ear, purposely trying to get under your skin. They love getting under your skin.

The people around them won't understand it. They will ask you why you're being this way, why did you react this way, what is your problem….but what they don't realize is; the covert narcissist is purposely pulling the strings in disguise. They will prod you, prod you, prod you and prod you until you snap. Don't let them get to you. You need to control your emotions against these monsters.

A covert narcissist wants to elicit control over every part of their life. Their social interactions, the things they watch, the places they go. This is relatively normal behavior for most people, but it goes a step further with a covert narcissist. They want to control people's emotions. They want to control the people around them and their feelings. Whether its acts of rage, sadness, confusion or lust – a covert wants you to react. A covert narcissist wants people to be reacting to things of their doing. They will set a social trap for you to fall in and they will watch from afar as you struggle. Like a damsel in distress, they will hide in the background and claim no responsibility; all they will do is sheepishly moan about their own life.

They love playing the victim. They love playing that fake violin in their life so people can feel sorry for them. "Men don't love me,", "I'm single," "I'm not good at anything," Whine, whine and whine. Spare me the story.

Though, ironically, even though they have a self deprecating humor; they still do like to think they are the best at everything. It's crazy.

They will think they are the strongest, the most talented, the most cunning, the most intelligent, the most beautiful, the most rational and the wisest. They think they are the best. If anyone gives them the reality check they need, that's when they will emotionally try to control you. That's when narcissistic rage will come in to effect. They love controlling people. More so, they love controlling people's emotions.


**Triangulation**
The very crux of Triangulation is that there are three parties involved (who form the 'triangle'). All three parties suffer from the

situation created by the narcissist. This can include the narcissist, his wife and his lover. Or, the narcissist, her victim and her close friends. Basically, what is happening is the Covert Narcissist is abusing his/her victim; this happens in such ways that at times the victims believe they themselves are at fault. Covert narcissists are so good at playing the victim; they will blame *their* victim for behaving out of line. Sadly, the abused will start to believe it and will react accordingly, most probably with guilt and regret. On the flipside, the Narcissist is conducting a calculated smear campaign on their victim, this completes the triangle. The person (or group) receiving the 'gossip' start having a negative perception of the victim. They then start to act aggressively towards the victim. This is the crux of triangulation. A vicious, unfortunate triangle, where the entities involved are manipulated to behave in a way controlled by the narcissist.

This is an extremely damaging and soul destroying act. Sadly, every covert narcissist will do this. If they ever feel threatened, they will go on attack mode, blame their victim and unleash a smear campaign. They believe they are being defensive when they psychologically harm someone. They actually believe they are the victim and that the real victim is being the bully.

Some people have asked in my Youtube videos if they are a narcissist. I truly believe a narcissist can't be saved, because they could never admit they are a narcissist in the first place.

A narcissist will never take responsibility for the abuse they inflict. In fact, they rationalize everything so convincingly in their own mind. They genuinely believe *they* are the victim. They can't stand themselves, but they will never admit any wrong doing. They believe they are being on the defensive.

One tell tale sign is the things they say to you. They tend to say to you what they think of themselves. "You're so negative", "You are emotionally shallow," "You're not a real man/woman".

A covert narcissist, deep inside, is a scared child. They are not rich in emotional depth. You won't see them crying at someone's pain, or to an emotional movie or to a song that reminds them of a loved one. They lack empathy.

They will push their own personality traits onto other people and then punish *them* for it. They are abusing themselves by proxy. What makes triangulation even more difficult is there is a third person to this. This makes up the 'triangle'. The narcissist will manipulate people so they can believe the actions of the victim are to be condemned. This then leads that person/group to be bullies in their own right. By attacking, accusing and smearing the victim's reputation.

This is triangulation; a vicious triangle where everyone is affected, emotionally and psychologically. All the while, the covert narcissist is the person behind it.

**Lies and Sex**

A covert narcissist is a pathological liar. They may have become a narcissist as a defense mechanism through a childhood trauma, abuse or a past experience that has left them broken. However this is viewed a person isn't just born this way. It's not autism – this is covert narcissism. These people love controlling people, they do it consciously. They're so accustomed to it; they will lie straight to your face and won't bat an eyelid. They are sick pathological liars.

One of the ways they can control people is through sex. Covert narcissists want everyone to be crazy about them. It's a narcissistic supply they can't get enough of. A covert narcissist is sexually extremely deviant. Not just by way of cheating, lying and playing people against each other. They are not loyal, they are cheaters and they will do the craziest things like sleeping with their best friend's partner – and somehow explaining their actions and still being the 'innocent one'. They are very good at controlling people and finding excuses. Sadly, their victims and the people around them believe everything they say and do.

Covert narcissists are extremely perverse individuals. Nothing is off limits to a covert narcissist. They hate themselves, so they will wish to illicit strong control in the  bedroom – anything you can think of, a covert narcissist will want to do it. On the flipside, they also have a God complex, a sense of entitlement, so they will believe they are entitled to anything to they want in the bedroom – hence, can play multiple roles.

It's all about **control**. They want to control every aspect of their life – even their perverse side. Covert narcissist's feel like the World owes them something. They will use people and discard of them like last weeks trash. They will use you, emotionally and physically and then kick you out onto the street. Only to find a new victim. **Control** is what motivates a covert narcissist in every way.

# CHAPTER 3
## EXCERPT FROM "THE DEVIL IN I"
## (PATTERNS & LOVE BOMBING)

Years on, I find myself in my New York apartment thinking of the impact Narko had on the world around us. As I look at my reflection I see nothing more than a shell of a human. My eyes are blank and my soul is empty. I have no identifiable human emotion apart from jealousy, lust and greed. Even when the Earth is given to me I am not satisfied. I can never be satisfied. Nothing can cure me. This is the price I have to pay.

Just like Narcissus did when looking at his reflection in the pond; his self-image destroyed him, and it destroyed the people around him. Just like the story of Snow White; The Queen was so obsessed with being the 'fairest of them all', she eventually lost everything; her fate was sealed.

Understanding a narcissist is to understand the meaning of true evil. The cunningness and intelligence of these creatures holds no limits; they are immaculately organized, sharp and fully aware of their surroundings. They are empty inside, an endless pit of depression, doom and loneliness. The irony is as empty as they are they are also very smart. One cannot beat a narcissist. You cannot outwit a narcissist. They are always ten steps ahead of you.

As complex as their games are and the spectrum of their personalities; they all follow a simple pattern when interacting with human beings; this can be dissected into three simple phases.

Phase one is what is known as the Over Evaluation Phase (often referred to as Love Bombing). Narcissists will begin by putting you on a pedestal. They will praise you: Your looks, your style, your intellect and your talents. They will give you a lot of attention to the point you a) enjoy the praise and b) become dependent on them, emotionally. They use a technique called 'mirroring', which is a psychological tactic to give the illusion you are a long lost friend of theirs. Don't be fooled by this. Well, actually, if any of this makes sense to you, you've already been caught up in the web. The victim will fall in love with the narcissist or at least build a strong emotional attachment to them, but it's probably love.

Narcissists don't know how to be normal, they struggle to interact. They have a lot of shallow relationships and probably hundreds of 'friends'. Most of these people, certainly the ones they interact with, are people they can control. These 'friends' often heap constant praise on the narcissist, giving them their much needed supply of self- gratification. If you don't heap praise or attention on this person, you won't have any chance of being in their circle: Which leads onto phase two.

This is what is known as the Devaluation Phase. This is when the narcissist gets bored of you and takes everything away. This is a sign of power, manipulation and control. They will suddenly stop heaping praise on you and leave you thinking, "What just happened?" This leaves victims confused, angry, and sad. This is the dark side of narcissists; the evil side. They have nothing in their life other than having people dependent on them so they seek to control it. They have used you for their own self-gratification and have thrown you out like yesterday's trash. They see people as nothing more than a source of praise, the 'narcissistic supply'.

After phase two, if you are not suicidal, depressed, or on the brink of insanity, you may wish to confront the narcissist. This is as good as signing a death wish. If the narcissist is confronted or challenged, they will move to Phase Three: Destroying You.

This will often take the form of a carefully constructed smear campaign. They will defame you and do everything to destroy your reputation. Nothing is off limits for these monsters; they will do and say anything to destroy you. They are patient. They will stalk you, prowl, and obsess over you, waiting for the exact moment to pounce. They will appear perfect, problem free, and they will even play the role of the victim themselves. The people around them will continue to shower them with praise and sympathy. Physically and emotionally, the narcissist will appear flawless, and it is all part of their act. Life is just a game to them.

A deadly smear campaign is easy for the narcissist to achieve because they always surround themselves with people they can control. These people will be caught up in their façade, their web of lies. They will believe everything the narcissist says, without question or hesitation.

The overt types are outgoing and confident, but the covert narcissists are shy. This is typically because they are too insecure to build a false grandiose self so they live in isolation. They create an inner world for themselves to live out their pathological fantasies.

Both types are equally dangerous. They are psychopaths. They will appear vulnerable in front of you, telling you sob stories of how their lives are so bad. But make no mistake, the drama is fake. They don't want sympathy; sympathy would insinuate you are above them. All they want is attention.

The paradox inside these evils is hard to understand, and it is why I write this now. To help you understand the mind of the soulless. Their minds are such they feel they are not good enough for anything, but at the same time truly believe they are the best at everything. They are not confident at anything, but at the same time, feel completely entitled. It is a completely ridiculous paradox and should not make sense, but it's exactly how these people feel. They are prone to self-isolation, self-pity and depression but all the while ensuring they are the centre of attention: A masterful skill in itself.

They see everyone as puppets and control everyone around them. They hate themselves and are ashamed of who they are; they can't bear the thought of being exposed and if remotely exposed, they will seek to destroy you. Challenging a narcissist is a deadly proposition and usually ends in the chaos and destruction of everyone around them. Lives will be ruined. Homes will be wrecked, and victims will have permanent, long lasting mental disorders.

*The Devil In I is available now on Amazon*

# CHAPTER 4
# HOW TO COPE WITH
# NARCISSISTIC ABUSE

Coping with narcissistic abuse is one of the hardest things you can do. It can take years to pick up the pieces and get your life back the way you want it. What makes it more difficult is no one around the narcissist seems to understand what has happened. It's difficult to discuss it with anyone. Narcissistic abuse is so discrete, so disguised, so covert, often no one around you or the narcissist can see it. At times, even the abused doesn't realize they are being abused until years later.

One thing to always remember is you are not alone. There are people out there in a similar position to you. One of the best things you can do is join the online communities, get active on the message boards and reach out to people who have experienced, or are experiencing similar things to you. There is a lot that can be achieved by discussing your story with people who understand.

If you are in a position where you are still in contact with the abuser there is one thing you can do to improve things. Go No Contact. This is very important. You can't waste your time trying to reason with a narcissist, they will always twist things and make you feel like you are paranoid or crazy. Going No Contact is the best way to start rebuilding your life.

A narcissist will do everything they can to get you out of the No Contact stage. They will laugh at you; make jokes that you are 'running away' and they will even twist it to suggest *they* are the ones going no contact from *you*. Don't give in to it. Stay true to yourself. The only way you can rebuild from narcissistic abuse is to go complete No Contact.

It's important to seek professional help to help you heal. If you feel you've suffered trauma, you may be suffering from PTSD (post traumatic stress disorder). This is an often disguised condition, but if you feel you have the following symptoms, you might be best speaking to a professional who can help you pave a path to recovery:-

- DepressionAnxiety
- Anger, a short temper Low libido
- Lack of sleep
- Nihilistic view of the world
- Giving up on your dreams and aspirations Low self esteem
- Low confidence
- Specific sights and sounds triggering strong emotional responses.

There are more symptoms I'm sure, but these are just a few. If you feel you have a few of these things. It might be best to speak to someone for professional help.

There is no one way to recover from narcissistic abuse, but getting your life back is important. Perhaps you can join a club, start a hobby, get active, set goals, and do things in your life that builds your confidence.

Meet new people, discover new things, and go to new places. Focus your energy onto positive things.

You know what the best revenge is against a narcissist? Happiness. They hate that you're happy. S.A.H, Successful, Ambitious and Happy. These three things are poison to a narcissist.

Don't worry about whether they know what you're doing or not. They will find everything out. They are the ultimate stalkers and spies. So, don't give them anything negative to latch on to. Be positive, keep winning, and get that smile back.

There is a lot of life in you and don't let the narcissist take that away from you.

# CHAPTER 5
# WHAT IS NARCISSISTIC RAGE?

Narcissistic Rage comes out when the narcissist is challenged. If you confront the malignant narcissist on something they have done that is selfish, damaging to an unfortunate recipient, or in any way morally wrong, they will see this as a challenge to their fake self. Any criticism will be met with the most violent of rage. Physically or verbally.

What are they capable of? The covert narcissist is a complete coward, so they will do everything in an indirect way. Firstly, they will tell their significant other, their work colleagues, their close friends, their family members of 'how cruel you are', 'how you attacked them' and 'how much damage you have caused them'. They will character assassinate you - like cowards, they will manipulate the people around them (who believe everything the narcissist says) to further their cause.

Once your character has been destroyed, they will look to damage your life. They are capable of everything and anything. If you look at them with anger, they will accuse you of being 'a woman beater'. The covert narcissist has no limits. They will call the police on you for something minor. They will try to destroy you and they will take you the edge of your life. They will make you suicidal.

Can you defend yourself? No. They are incredible at hiding. You cannot defend yourself or in any way attack them. They have too much control of the people around them.

Narcissistic rage is quite possibly the most dangerous thing on the planet. They are incredibly clever beings; a covert narcissist will ensure to cover their steps. They are near untraceable. They will plot and meticulously plan an attack that will have lasting damage.

Can you see narcissistic rage? Well, yes. An overt will openly fight you, will openly attack. A covert is more cunning, but still dangerous. you can see when the mask slips!

If you say or do anything that exposes a narcissist, you will see a look in their eyes that is pure evil. This is often known as the 'narcissistic stare'. When you see this stare, run for the hills.

The best way to handle a covert narcissistic is to have NO CONTACT. I've mentioned this a few times throughout this eBook because it's so important to your survival. NO CONTACT means NO CONTACT. You can't defeat these people. You can't beat them. You can't win. Cut all contact.

They will do things to try and smoke you out and have you back in their lab rat game that they call life. They will say things like, 'Oh you're turning your back on your family!', 'How cold of you to never want see your nieces and nephews again!', 'All you do is run!', 'You're just a baby!'

These are things to turn the tables back on you. Remember, the narcissist is a liar, they hide, they are manipulators and they have no empathy. They never apologize and are always blaming others for their shortfalls. You cannot beat a narcissistic. They are control freaks and can't bear the thought of anyone holding the higher moral ground on them.

They are extremely jealous and vengeful people. Narcissistic rage has no limits. If you do anything to make the mask slip, the true colours of the malignant narcissist will be revealed - and what's under there, their true colours, is evil, cold and extremely dangerous.

221

# CHAPTER 6
## GASLIGHTING

Gaslighting is something covert narcissists do to manipulate the conditions around their victim, making you question your own sanity. You will literally be driven to insanity whilst in the presence of a covert narcissist. They are incredible liars.

The term comes from a 1944 movie called *Gaslight* (though it was originally made in 1940 before Hollywood picked it up in 1944). The movie is about a husband and wife, in which the husband attempts to drive the wife insane. He starts moving things in the house, and when she questions him about it, he denies it. Things flicker on the wall, and when she asks him about it, he says nothing is flickering. She slowly loses her mind.

This is quite an extreme example, but Covert Narcissists will make you go insane. For example, a malignant covert narcissist will flirt with you to no end and create the illusion that something may be happening. She will then take that away, leaving you confused. It's things like this that will make you question whether what was happening before was real. Narcissists make you question yourself. They make you question reality.

The covert narcissist will verbally berate you, abuse you, and make you feel so low. But at the same time, they will say, 'YOU are a crazy', 'YOU are a psychopath!', 'YOU are selfish', and 'YOU have no future'. You are being attacked from every angle. Not only are you being bullied and abused, but you are being told you are the one in the wrong with psychological issues. Narcissists will cast their own traits, their own feelings and their own insecurities onto you. This will make you question yourself. No matter if 99% of the people in your life have a strong relationship with you, with enriched conversations and empowering ambitions - the covert narcissist will keep berating you and try to convince you of something different.

What makes this even crazier is, they do this all in a disguised way. They will hide it by saying, 'I'm saying this because I care for you', 'I want you to get help', 'I really hope you see a shrink', 'I care for you so much and want you to get better'. They make you question your sanity. A covert narcissist will sooner drive someone into an insane asylum than to offer constructive advice. They are incapable of humble heartwarming motivational pep talk. They will never extend their hand out to you. They will only offer you a poisoned chalice.

Gaslighting can come in many forms. Women or men will flirt with you, make you love them and then step away, making you question yourself. "What did I do wrong?", "Was it something I said?" and when you question the covert narcissist, they will play the victim, "Stop harassing me!", "We were only talking as friends!", "You're crazy".

It's very difficult to understand if you're being gaslighted because it is disguised so well. It happens over time. You are abused and after a year you will ask yourself, "Am I being abused?" You won't even know it.

One thing I will say is, if you have an uneasy feeling about someone or something, listen to it! Your subconscious is far more active and is picking up on things your conscious mind is not aware of. You need to listen to your gut instinct. It is a powerful tool. Our brains are extremely advanced - it operates on multiple levels. Listen to your gut instinct.

# CHAPTER 7
## LOVING A NARCISSIST

Loving a covert narcissist is a very easy thing to do. On the surface, they are the 'perfect being'. They are so good at disguising their inner feelings, insecurities and motives it can often take years to know you've been in the presence of a covert narcissist. A lot of people have shared their stories on my YouTube channel of how after 20+ years of marriage, they finally realized their husband or wife is a covert narcissist. I have had similar experiences, also.

The covert narcissist will abuse you, stomp on your self-esteem, and destroy you mentally, but it will take years for you to realize. You will actually ask yourself, 'What is going on here?'

If you do fall in love with a narcissist, it is very difficult to get out of that web. Like a White Widow spider they will wrap you in their web of evil - it's very difficult to get out.

As I mentioned in the previous chapter, they will Gaslight you, they will manipulate the environment around you and then make you question whether YOU are insane. Covert Narcissists will openly accuse you of being 'a psycho', 'a crazy', 'paranoid', 'out of control' - they are simply exerting their own insecurities and feelings onto you.

When you love someone, you start to make excuses for them. You start to ignore their downfalls, you start to accept their flaws;

you see their dark sides as quirkiness. Which is fine, this is what love is. Love is all about accepting someone for who they are. This is why it's even harder to reveal and expose a narcissist if you're in love with them. At this point, you'd be too far down the rabbit hole. Too far in.

You will make excuses for them and won't be objective. Love is a selfless thing.

This is a good starting point to figure out if you are in love with a covert narcissist. Ask yourself, what is this person giving me? Are they doing anything selfless for me? If someone is in love with someone, they will travel the earth for that person; they will drop everything and go to their aid. The phone will always be on for them. They won't prioritize other things over you - they will always make time for you. They will actually arrange their diary TO fit you in, not the other way around.

Covert Narcissists are addicted to narcissistic supply. So if you're worshiping them, they will keep you close, which in turn may give you the illusion that they love you back. They don't. They are being selfish. Ask yourself an honest question: What is this person doing for me? Are they doing something for a motive? Are they doing something to show they care? Are they asking how I'm feeling? Do they care for you? Do they do spontaneous things to surprise you and make you feel good? Do they include you in their future plans?

A covert narcissist is great at faking things; they can sometimes make grand plans for marriage after just a few days of meeting you! (Yes, that's how crazy they are). As mentioned in the previous chapter of *The Devil In I* excerpt - they have the over-evaluation phase in which they will shower you with compliments and make you addicted to the attention. This is also referred to as Love Bombing. However, what they will do is take it all away with the De-Evaluation phase (then it's the complete destruction phase).

Be careful. The covert narcissist is always playing games. They can create great illusions. They are manipulative and great liars. Great control freaks.

By the time you've noticed it, it may be too late - your heart is dictating you.

One thing I will say is research from multiple sources and try to be objective in your analysis. It's not easy. It can take years to get over your malignant narcissist. Over time, you will remember only the 'good' things but will forget the endless torment they inflicted on you. Don't go back. Always remember the pain.

You have to go No Contact if you feel you have a Narcissist in your life. They are dangerous, evil, and extremely influential.

Loving a covert narcissist will end badly. I can't envision a happy ending with these individuals.

Get help from a professional, talk with friends, analyze from several sources, and try to get your life back. Start hobbies, make new friends, and create goals in your life. There are more people in the world. You need to realize they are Pure Evil, just complete scumbag monsters. Don't let your heart out so easily. Analyze what they do for you and be vocal about it.

There is no easy answer to this, but loving a narcissist is an easy thing to do. In some ways, you will enable them, and it will become a vicious circle.

# CHAPTER 8
# WHY ARE NARCISSISTS
# THE WAY THEY ARE?

This is a question that unfortunately this author cannot answer. There are several theories out there that can be considered. Is it a case of nature or nurture? Is the covert born this way or have they developed this mask over time?

I personally think it is a combination of both, but I'd like to lean more toward the 'nurture' theory. I'd like to think every human is born innocent.

Perhaps it is years of abuse that leads the narcissist to build walls around themselves. Perhaps they created the mask to hide vulnerabilities, as a defense mechanism to life.

Maybe they are naturally nihilistic due to how they have been treated in life. Insecurities they have picked up through abuse may be contributing factors. Depression may have led them to build a fake self.

Some people believe they are born with a deficiency. Something missing inside of them genetically that doesn't allow them to feel empathy. This may be the case, but unlike psychopaths, I believe narcissists know what they are doing! When they gaslight, when they manipulate, when they wield their power to undermine people and destroy reputations. I truly believe the narcissist is aware of what they are doing. It's not completely innate, they are responsible for their actions.

Perhaps the world in which they grew up in was so unbearable they needed to create something different to survive. Whatever the case may be, they are complete monsters. The truest of all evil. I truly believe a covert narcissist is the most self-righteous, evil, selfish, arrogant, and manipulative scumbag on the planet. Money, status, and power are important to the narcissist, but if you look closely, they haven't achieved any of these things. It's all fake. You can see a covert narcissist's true colours by looking over the facade. Others around them may have some form of 'status' or 'money' - but they themselves will not.

I truly believe a person's contribution to this world is judged by how charitable they are, how helpful they are to others and how passionate they are to making change in the world. Steve Jobs, Walt Disney, and Elon Musk - all these people have made huge changes. Philanthropists are the world's giants who must be celebrated. Psychiatrists, teachers, and doctors - these are the people who must be celebrated. Are they helping others? Are they doing things to enrich people's lives?

The covert narcissists I know do NONE of these things. They simply consume life; they take from life and stomp on people's self-esteem. They are the ultimate bullies, but conversely, they are the ultimate cowards.

# CHAPTER 9
## ARE YOU A NARCISSIST?

It's very difficult to know if you are Covert Narcissist. True narcissists don't realize they have anything wrong with them. They fully justify their actions. Everything they do is rationalized in their twisted reality.

When anyone says, 'I think I am a narcissist', then I am instantly suspicious. Narcissists, may it be covert, overt, or malignant, are extremely intelligent people (though not as much as they think they are). They are smart enough to know their actions may be scrutinized, so they disguise their true colors very well. They are not oblivious to their social status, in fact, they are very aware of it. This makes them incredibly dangerous.

Covert Narcissists are not frequent users of social media - if anything they barely post! An overt would post all the time, parading his or hers 'perfect' life. But a Covert may not even have Facebook. They live in their own reality and will hide as much as possible. If they have Facebook, it's simply to spy on others and keep track of anything that can harm people's reputations.

Do you think you are you a covert narcissist? It's hard to know. But one way of finding out if you are a narcissist is to discover if you have empathy! Narcissists lack empathy - and if they do, they'll fake it. If you do this test and are completely honest about it, you'll reveal whether you have empathy and what truly motivates you as a person.

**The Empathy Test**

I want you to imagine a genie. You rub a lamp and a genie comes out. The genie comes out and says, "I will give you a Millions Dollars!"

"A million dollars?" you ask.

"Yes, a million dollars", the genie says. So he writes you a cheque and he extends his arm. Before you get it, he says, "No. Before you get this cheque. I want you to do something".

"What can I do?" you ask the genie.

"If you take this cheque, you have to give me permission to kill 10 people in your neighbourhood", he explains.

So, here you are confronted with your first scenario. You are offered One Million dollars but 10 people in your neighbourhood will die.

Now, a narcissist may rationalize this and say, 'Ok, I'm not the one killing these people' or he may say, 'people die every single day. What difference does it make if it's in my own neighbourhood or not?'

So, what do you do?

The genie changes the stakes, he says, "The 10 people in your neighbourhood are people you know. You will have spoken to these people on several occasions, in the local mall, the local store, the local garage, the local school".

So, now there is an emotional connection. Do you take the million dollars?

I don't know how you're answering these, but the genie makes it extra difficult.

"I will give you the million dollars, and ten people in your neighbourhood of whom you are aware of will die. But I want you to do one more thing. Each of the ten people that die will have kids under the age of 10. Once you take the money, you need to sit face to face with each of the children and explain to them why their parents are dead, and you can't lie!"

What do you do?

Now, no one with empathy would take the money. Personally, I could never imagine doing it.

What do you do?

This is only a simple test to see if you have empathy or not. This by no means defines whether you're a narcissist, but it gets you a step closer to revealing whether you're a narcissist, or a psychopath, or someone who lacks empathy.

**The Room Game**

The following 'game' is not a test to see if you are a covert narcissist. There is no 'one' way to find out if someone is a covert narcissist. However, there are a number of techniques to help you paint the picture.

The following game will appear to have no meaning to the person with whom you are doing it. If you tell them the purpose of the game, the covert will react to it and will try to manipulate their answers. You need to present this game as a fun game with no meaning, and encourage honest answers.

So here it is: Imagine a room. In that room, imagine a table. Where is the table? What does the table look like?

Now imagine a ladder. Where is the ladder? What does the ladder look like?

Imagine a vase. Where is the vase? Are there any flowers in the vase? If so, how many? Imagine a horse. Where is the horse? What does the horse look like?

Now, imagine a storm in the room. What happens to all the things in the room?

This is a test that is in one of my YouTube videos, and the answers from those who have commented have been really interesting! Almost all of them are different. It just shows how different everyone's brains work.

What does the test mean? Well, the table is a representation of you. If you have a Big Oak table in the centre of the room - this would suggest you are centred, grounded and extremely confident.

How does this link to covert narcissism? The Covert will not imagine such a thing. They inherently hate themselves, so their table will be small, weak structured and perhaps in the corner of the room.

The Ladder represents your ambitions. A strong tall ladder propped up against the wall is a sign you are ambitious and forward thinking.

The covert narcissist may be ambitious or defeatist, but I'm unsure if they'd have a tall strong ladder. Someone with a sideways ladder on the floor would suggest someone with a feeling of hopelessness.

The vase with flowers is a sign of your family and friends. A Vase with lots of flowers would suggest you have a lot of friends that you hold dear to you. If it's on the table (you) it would further this view.

A covert narcissist would have no flowers, maybe just one.

The Horse is representative of your spouse. Oddly enough, women tend to imagine a big stallion, whilst men would imagine a pony. If your spouse is strong, he/she will be close to the table.

A covert narcissist may have the horse outside, or perhaps looking away from the table, looking outside. Or, if the covert is living vicariously through someone who is 'successful', then the horse may be close to the table.

The storm is representative of what happens to all of those elements in times of turmoil.

Some people with a negative outlook would have everything destroyed, even themselves. The table, ladder, horse, and flowers will all fall apart (you think they'd all flee in times of trouble).

But a strong independent person with good friends would have all those elements standing strong after turmoil.

Let me point out - this game is not a 'narcissist' test. And some people may not believe in this type of thing. If you're open to the subconscious brain, if you believe the subconscious harnesses more answers about ourselves, then this test is for you. If you don't believe that, then this test is lost on you. Take it with a pinch of salt, but try the test. Analyze your answers. Does it ring true with you? Is it an accurate perception of who you are and how you see those things in your life? Only you will truly know the answer to these questions.

# ACKNOWLEDGEMENTS

Thank you so much for reading this book, it means a lot to me and I sincerely hope the contents and ideas expressed in these pages have helped you in some way. If there is just one idea that has helped you, then it will have been a success for me. Please keep sharing what you know about narcissistic abuse, covert narcissism and psychological bullying. It is still considered a niche topic and it requires everyones collective efforts to keep shining a light on these destructive behavioural patterns. Keep communicating with your friends, family and social network to get the red flags out there. Once again, thank you for being part of this journey, and if you ever have any questions please find me on my website or social media and I will try my best to help. Many thanks. Keep going.